ORLANDO

Orlando

SALLY POTTER

based on the book by

VIRGINIA WOOLF

faber and faber
LONDON · BOSTON

First published in 1994
by Faber and Faber Limited
3 Queen Square London WCIN 3AU

Photoset in Linotype Plantin by Parker Typesetting Service, Leicester
Printed in England by Clays Ltd, St Ives plc

© Sally Potter, 1994

Photos from *Orlando* by Liam Longman © Adventure Pictures,
except photo on page 59
© Chris Steele-Perkins (Magnum Photos)

Sally Potter is hereby identified as author of this work in
accordance with Section 77 of the Copyright, Designs and Patents Act 1988

A CIP record for this book
is available from the British Library

ISBN 0–571–17295–4

6 8 10 9 7 5

Contents

Acknowledgements

Film-making is a collaborative art form. And whilst writing is essentially a solitary activity there are always hidden others who play crucial roles in the process of script development.

Thanks must go to British Screen and the European Script Fund, who provided financial support for the scriptwriting. Among the many individuals who played a part, I would particularly like to thank Tilda Swinton for her dedicated energy, intelligent suggestions and the intense and sometimes hilarious working sessions we shared over the four-year development period; Simon Perry of British Screen for his timely and acute comments; Alexandra Cann, my agent, for her indefatigable loyalty; Walter Donohue, my story editor, for his subtle, precise encouragement and criticism; Roanne Moore, for typing and re-typing my handwritten pages with astonishing speed and accuracy; and Christopher Sheppard, my producer, without whose tireless commitment, support and ingenuity this film could not have been made.

Finally, this screenplay could only exist because of Virginia Woolf's book. I hope she will forgive the liberties I have taken with her inspiring work.

Alexei Rodionov using steadicam with Sally Potter on the left, St Petersburg.

INTRODUCTION

When I first read *Orlando* as a teenager, I remember quite clearly the experience of *watching* it in my mind's eye, as if it were a film. The experience was visual, even if the book was cloaked in literary reference. Throughout my twenties, when I was involved primarily in theatre, dance and performance art, the book remained as a reference point and source of inspiration, both conscious and unconscious. *Orlando* became a personal catchword for work that dared to be epic, non-realistic and completely believable in its own terms.

By the time I came to write my first treatment of *Orlando* in 1984, I felt as though the film already existed; I just needed to look intently enough with my inner eye and write down what I could see. And thus began a long journey. I wrote the first screenplay in 1988. Four years and many drafts later the cameras turned on the ice in St Petersburg.

The process of adaptation was, of course, not as simple as I had anticipated. But my first instinct – that the book worked primarily through imagery, and was therefore eminently cinematic – was affirmed in Virginia Woolf's diaries where she writes of her attempt with *Orlando* to 'exteriorise consciousness'. In other words, she set out to find images rather than abstract literary monologues to describe the secret machinery of the mind in such a way that the outer world – with its weather, costume and surfaces of all kinds – became an expression of inner complexity.

At the time of first publication, this led some critics to dismiss *Orlando* as one of Virginia Woolf's more lightweight books (though the public loved it). The critics failed to appreciate her ironical overview of English history and the powerful ideas embedded in its imagery.

But when I came to write the screenplay, Virginia Woolf's intentions and the spirit of the book did not, in fact, leap naturally onto the page. On the contrary, the deeper I went, the more I realized I would have to be prepared to make changes – ruthless changes if necessary – in order to stay true to what I loved in the book, and yet enable it to work as a film.

I set about this in the usual ways: reading and re-reading the book, her other novels and diaries – in fact *anything* pertaining to *Orlando* and its genesis (including Virginia Woolf's own sources); then writing and re-writing the treatment, a step outline, and finally successive drafts of the screenplay. I made endless diagrammatic plots to help strip things back to the bone, find the guiding principles, and reconstruct the story from the inside out.

As I was a relative beginner at telling stories, this process was both uncomfortable and educative. I grew up as part of an aesthetic movement that was all about taking stories apart and looking at the lies that conventional storytelling might tell. But with *Orlando* I found myself falling in love with narrative. The journey of adaptation became a vehicle for learning – not just about history, costume and literature – but also about storytelling itself and the search for the essential. Because *Orlando* the book breaks so many rules, dances through so many literary forms, and plays with such thematic complexity, my task became one of simplification: narratively, thematically and structurally. Although the book was already a distillation of 400 years of English history (albeit an imagined history told with a liberal amount of poetic licence) the film needed to distil even further.

In the last year of writing, on the advice of my story editor Walter Donohue, I put the book away entirely and treated the script as something in its own right, as if the book had never existed. By that stage, I had to trust that I knew it well enough not to lean on it any more; that to be slavish to the book would be a disservice to it; and that just as Virginia Woolf was a writer committed to writing and constantly exploring the form of the novel itself, so I now needed to dedicate myself to the energy of cinema. The screenplay would have no pretensions of literary merit – indeed, one of my first ruthless tasks was to divest it of redundant literary concerns. The screenplay needed to become a 'lean, mean machine' (to quote Spike Lee), a technical document which had already had all the necessary uncomfortable questions asked of it and would be sturdy enough to carry a cast and crew through its making.

The most fundamental changes were structural. The story line was simplified and events which did not significantly further Orlando's story were dropped. Also, the narrative needed to be driven. Whereas the novel could withstand abstraction and arbitrariness (such as Orlando's change of sex), cinema is more pragmatic. There had to be reasons – however flimsy – to propel us along a journey based, itself, on a kind of suspension of disbelief. Thus, in the film it is Queen Elizabeth who bestows Orlando's long life upon him ('Do not fade, do not wither, do not grow old . . .') whereas in the book it remains unexplained. And Orlando's change of sex in the film is a result of his having reached a crisis point – a crisis of masculine identity. On the battlefield he looks death and destruction in the face and confronts the challenge of kill or be killed. It is Orlando's unwillingness to conform to what is expected of him as a man that leads – within the logic of the film – to his change of sex. Later, as a woman, Orlando finds that she cannot conform to what is expected of her as a female either, and makes a series of choices which leave her, unlike in the book, without marriage or property – and with a daughter, not a son.

These latter changes seemed to me entirely consistent with Virginia Woolf's views in her other works on the condition of women's lives (especially *A Room Of One's Own*) and crisply logical within the framework she had set up in the earlier part of the story.

Orlando was, of course, originally written as a spoof biography of Vita Sackville-West. It seemed to me that where the book held most tightly to apparent biographical facts, it occasionally tended to lose its power as a story (such as Orlando's 'keeping' the house at the end of the book – which was a way for Virginia Woolf to restore the lost Knole to Vita Sackville-West). So I decided to 'disentangle' the film from its biographical references, which also permitted a more biting and satirical view of the English class system and the colonial attitudes arising from it.

At the same time I needed to ensure that Orlando was a loveable character. The clue was to highlight Orlando's essential innocence. He happens to have been born into a class, a place and a time – by which he is shaped – but as the times and circumstances change, so he/she changes also. The essential human remains: the patterns of behaviour and attitude are transformed. In this way, Orlando's loss of property and status in the twentieth century takes on a different significance. Whilst Orlando's disinheritance is a symptom of the second-class status of women, there is also an aspect which is worthy of celebration: the loss of privilege and status based on an outdated English class system.

I also decided to give Orlando's love affair with Shelmerdine a rather different significance. It is impossible to think about the twentieth century without acknowledging the role of the USA in world affairs. For this reason I decided to make Shelmerdine an American, and give him the voice of the new world – the romantic and revolutionary view of the beginning of the American Dream. Their paths cross at the dawn of the Industrial Revolution and at the height of gothic romanticism. Shelmerdine functions as the one looking to the future while Orlando is apparently still trapped in the past. In the book Orlando's marriage with Shelmerdine loosely envelops the last part of the story. In the film they meet and then definitively part. Orlando's story does not end in the arms of a romantic saviour but in accepting responsibility for her own life in the present.

And what of *additions* to the script? During the period of raising the finance for the film, the producer, Christopher Sheppard, and I went backwards and forwards many times between London and the former Soviet Union, meeting potential co-production partners, looking for locations, taking photographs, and so on. Some of these trips provided inspiration for new scenes in the script. For example, on one of the many trips to Uzbekhistan to try to set up the shooting there for the scenes Virginia Woolf had set in Constantinople, we were told that the most powerful man in town was the Mayor of Khiva (the walled city where we eventually made this section of the film), and that it was important to build a relationship before we really talked business. So we took him a stereo system and he took us out into the desert, where he had set a table covered in food and a lot of bottles of vodka under the burning sun. And there we stood – for hours – exchanging toasts: 'To your British film industry!' 'To the great film industry of Uzbekhistan!' 'To international co-operation in the name of cinema!' and so on. Night fell, we built a bonfire, and then we all sang to each other.

On the basis of this, Christopher Sheppard was able to sign at the end of the day – in a rather drunken condition – some hastily scribbled contracts, which became the basis of a deal. We were able to film in the ancient walled city where no other Western crew, to my knowledge, had ever done so. But in addition, the experience became a scene in the film. I went straight home, got out my pencil, and started writing. This became a constant process: feeding the experience of making the film back into the work itself.

And so the script progressed in parallel with raising money: the so-called 'development' of the film. One by one, obstacles were overcome, larger and larger loans were raised from the bank, the stakes got higher, and the possibility that the film might actually get made started to ignite some enthusiasm in otherwise cynical and negative investors.

But one question remained for many of them – why was *Orlando* relevant to today? How would a modern audience connect with the story? I searched for a form that would mirror my own conviction that the issues in the film were entirely pertinent, and that the *tone* of the book might itself provide a clue. For whilst it is a work that is melancholy at its heart, it is light and witty in its delivery.

I tried writing the whole screenplay in verse; I tried an intimate voiceover. And finally, with Tilda Swinton's help, I settled on Orlando's looks and addresses to camera. I wanted to convert Virginia Woolf's literary wit into a cinematic humour at which people could laugh out loud. I hoped that this direct address would create a golden thread that would connect the audience, through the lens, with Orlando, and that in this way the spectacle and the spectator would become one through the release of laughter.

But how else was this a story of now? The novel ends in 1928, but in order to keep faith with Virginia Woolf's use of real time in ending the novel (with the story finishing just as she puts down her pen to finish the book), the film had to end when it was completed – in 1992. I experimented with various endings during the writing stage, but the ending only reached its final form after everything else had been shot. What became clear was that the correct way to approach it was not just to stick an ending on to the story, but to attempt to think myself into Virginia Woolf's consciousness. What might she have done with the story had she lived until 1992? It was a strange game, a sort of second-guessing that consisted of my re-reading what she had written after

Orlando, trying to glean her thoughts on issues post-1928. It seemed clear that I had to refer to both the First and Second World Wars. And because the book itself is almost a running commentary on the history of literature as the vehicle of consciousness, there had to be a cinematic equivalent of what had happened to that kind of consciousness post-war, particularly through the arrival of the electronic age.

All these changes, and other smaller ones too (dropping characters and scenes, writing poems and dialogue from sometimes slender clues on the page) were really manifestations of one central drive, which was the drive towards the central meaning of the book – indeed, that which had attracted me to it in the first place. I wanted to eliminate the unnecessary, and saturate with meaning what remained.

To do this I knew that I needed to face at the script-writing stage questions that on previous films, to my cost, I had only faced in the cutting room. From work with live performance I knew the value of the dress rehearsal where you face the horrible reality of what you have got, when there is still the chance to make changes. I wanted to face that discomfort *before* shooting, not after. Even when the script was apparently finished and ready to go I kept asking myself the most difficult question: 'But what is this *really* about?'

The answers came slowly. It gradually seemed to me that *Orlando* was, at its heart, a celebration of impermanence. Through the vehicle of Orlando's apparent immortality we experience the mutability of all things and relationships. This brings with it both a sense of loss (of the past) and a feeling of joy (of a possible future). The film ends on a similar metaphysical note to the book, with Orlando caught somewhere between heaven and earth, in a place of ecstatic communion with the present.

But what of Orlando's change of sex, which provides the most extraordinary narrative twist, and was Virginia Woolf's rich and light way of dealing with issues between men and women? The longer I lived with Orlando and tried to write a character who was both male and female, the more ludicrous maleness and femaleness became, and the more the notion of the essential human being – that a man and woman both are – predominated.

Here was a character called Orlando: a person, an individual, a being who lived for 400 years, first as a man and then as a woman. At the moment of change, Orlando turns and says to the audience: 'Same person . . . different sex.' It is as simple as that.

Sally Potter
London
December 1993

ORLANDO

Front titles begin.
Cut to:

SCENE I: EXT. DAY. ENGLISH LANDSCAPE
An English landscape in late summer. ORLANDO *paces back and forth beneath an oak tree, holding a book. He is murmuring, looking at the book occasionally, learning some verse. He wears the clothes of a young Elizabethan man: doublet and hose, a ruff at his neck.*

ORLANDO: (*Voiceover*) There can be no doubt about his sex – despite the feminine appearance that every young man of the time aspires to. And there can be no doubt about his upbringing. Good food, education, a nanny, loneliness and isolation.
(ORLANDO *sits down at the base of the tree, puts down his book, and stares out at the landscape.*)
(*Voiceover*) And because this is England, Orlando would therefore seem destined to have his portrait on the wall and his name in the history books. But when he –
(ORLANDO *turns and looks into the camera.*)
(*To camera*) – that is, I –
(*He turns away as the voiceover continues.*)
(*Voiceover*) – came into the world, he was looking for something else. Though heir to a name which meant power, land and property, surely when Orlando was born it wasn't privilege he sought, but company.
(ORLANDO *picks up a parchment and quill as if to start writing, his hand hovering above the blank page, then puts it down with a sigh.*)
Cut to:

Front titles continue.
Cut to:

3

SCENE 2: EXT. DUSK. ENGLISH LANDSCAPE

ORLANDO *lies sprawled asleep at the foot of the oak tree. A distant trumpet call startles him awake and he jumps up and runs off across the fields.*

SCENE 3: EXT. DUSK. GREAT HOUSE AND GROUNDS AND RIVER

A high falsetto voice can be heard singing a song in honour of QUEEN ELIZABETH I *over the following sequence:*

Servants carrying flaming torches rush out of the huge doors in the entrance to a Great House.

Cut to:

Lines of oars cutting rhythmically into the dark river water.

Cut to:

ORLANDO *running up the front path and into the Great House, as the servants carrying flaming torches rush past him in the opposite direction.*

Cut to:

QUEEN ELIZABETH *in the royal barge. She perches stiffly, attentive courtiers on either side, as the oarsmen pull the boat through the water. On the riverbank servants are dashing about with flaming torches, the points of light reflected, glittering, in the water.*

Cut to:

A small, decorated boat is launched into the water. The falsetto stands in the boat, singing to the QUEEN *as she approaches.*

Cut to:

The Royal oarsmen lift their oars.

Cut to:

Close-up of QUEEN ELIZABETH'*s profile as her boat drifts past the singer and the glittering lights.*

Cut to:

Front titles conclude as the high male singing voice reaches its peak, echoing out over the water.

Cut to:

Servants bearing torches lining up in front of the Great House. Twinkling lights appear, one after the other in the windows. Then servants carrying torches appear along the roof-top until the outline of the house is etched in flames.

Cut to:

The back view of QUEEN ELIZABETH *leading a stately procession*

4

along the path towards the entrance of the house.
Cut to:
ORLANDO's PARENTS *hurrying out from the house through the torches
and fountains, looking back anxiously for their son.*
Cut to:
ORLANDO *frantically changing his clothes by flickering candlelight,
helped by three extremely anxious valets, who stroke, pull and pat*
ORLANDO's *shapely crimson doublet and hose into place.*
Cut to:
Close-up of ORLANDO's *legs as he leaps downstairs in shoes decorated
with rosettes.*
Cut to:
The front door of the Great House as it flies open and ORLANDO
dashes out and down the steps between the flames.
Cut to:
Close-up of ORLANDO *as a small bowl of rosewater is thrust into his
hands. He sinks onto his knees, breathing rapidly, holding out the
bowl, rose petals floating on the glinting surface of the water.*
Cut to:
*Close-up of the two Royal ringed hands descending into the water –
they are nervous, crabbed, sickly, imperious hands. The rings flash in
the light and water.*

Cut to the QUEEN's *face as she looks quizzically down at* ORLANDO. *His face is flushed, rosy in the flickering light of the torches, reflected from the bowl of rosewater.*
Cut to:
Caption:

1600
DEATH

Fade out.

SCENE 4: INT. NIGHT. GREAT HALL
The dark panelled banquet hall is lit by hundreds of candles; a fire blazes in the huge fireplace; a long polished table is covered entirely with orange and yellow sugared flowers.
QUEEN ELIZABETH *sits at the far end of the hall at the head of the table near the fire. She has pale eyes in a strained, whitened face and wears an orange wig. Her dress is elaborately jewelled and embroidered.* ORLANDO's PARENTS *sit attentively on either side of her; several courtiers are seated along the table, and at the opposite end sits* ORLANDO, *closely watching the* QUEEN.
ORLANDO's FATHER *signals to* ORLANDO, *who rises nervously to his feet and turns towards* QUEEN ELIZABETH, *who is staring fixedly at him, holding a sugared daffodil at her lips.*

6

ORLANDO *gestures extravagantly and starts to recite from 'The Faerie Queene'.*

ORLANDO: '. . . Ah, see the Virgin Rose, how sweetly she doth
   first peep forth with bashful modesty,
   That fairer seems, the less ye see her may . . .
   Lo see soon after, how more bold and free, her bared
      bosom she doth broad display . . .
   Lo see soon after how she fades, and falls away . . .'
   (QUEEN ELIZABETH *raises her hand and* ORLANDO *falters,
   then stops.*)

QUEEN ELIZABETH: Is this a worthy topic from one so clearly in
   the bloom of youth to one who would desire it still?
   (ORLANDO's FATHER *rises and bows to the* QUEEN.)

ORLANDO's FATHER: (*Tremulously*) Fair Virgo – Gracious
   Majesty – your . . . er . . . bloom is legendary and these, of
   course, were not the sentiments of our son, but of a poet.
   And now – what would please you? All that is mine is here
   for your pleasure.

QUEEN ELIZABETH: (*Sardonically*) All you call yours is mine
   already.
   (QUEEN ELIZABETH *now turns her gaze upon* ORLANDO, *who
   blushes as their eyes meet.*)

SCENE 5: EXT. DAY. THE GROUNDS

ORLANDO *and* QUEEN ELIZABETH *are walking in the grounds of the
house, with several dogs trotting beside them. Courtiers hover
watchfully in tight formation a few steps behind. Two courtiers carry a
heavy throne.*

Cut to:

QUEEN ELIZABETH *seated on the throne on the lawn, surrounded by
her courtiers.* ORLANDO *stands respectfully before her with his*
PARENTS *and the dogs.*

QUEEN ELIZABETH *gestures and an attendant places a velvet cushion
at her feet.*

QUEEN ELIZABETH: Come. Your leg.
   (ORLANDO *kneels on the cushion and tentatively lifts his knee
   towards her.*
   QUEEN ELIZABETH *bends stiffly to tie a jewelled Order of the
   Garter just below his knee, lingering there, lightly stroking his leg.*)

7

QUEEN ELIZABETH: I want you here. In England, with me. You
will be the son of my old age and the limb of my infirmity.
My favourite. My *mascot*.
(ORLANDO *stares up at her, wide-eyed.*)

SCENE 6: INT. NIGHT. CORRIDOR
ORLANDO *is hovering anxiously outside a bedroom door. The*
QUEEN *calls imperiously from within.*
QUEEN ELIZABETH: Come.
(ORLANDO *turns for a moment and looks into the camera – a look
of innocent trepidation – before disappearing through the door.*)

SCENE 7: INT. NIGHT. QUEEN ELIZABETH'S BEDROOM
Two female attendants are expertly helping the QUEEN *out of some of
the outer layers of her dress. We are aware of the heaviness and
stiffness of her jewel-encrusted garments.*
The attendants lower the QUEEN *gently onto the cushions of her bed,
curtsey deeply and then shuffle backwards out of the room. A fire
crackles. Wind whistles in the chimney.*
The QUEEN *beckons* ORLANDO *over and then gestures for him to join
her on the bed. As he tentatively clambers up bedside her, she pulls him
down, burying his face in her lap.*

8

QUEEN ELIZABETH: Ah. *This* is my victory.
> (ORLANDO *lies half smothered in the fabric, trying to breathe without moving too much.*
> *The* QUEEN *pulls* ORLANDO *up towards her and kisses his forehead sensually. He perches rather awkwardly beside her.*)
> Come, your handsome leg.
> (*The* QUEEN *reaches slowly into her bodice and pulls out a rolled parchment which she tucks – sensuously – into the garter just below his knee.*)
> For you. And for your heirs, Orlando. The house.

ORLANDO: (*Stumbling for words*) Your Majesty, I am forever in your debt . . .

QUEEN ELIZABETH: But on one condition. Do not fade. Do not wither. Do not *grow old.*

SCENE 8: INT. NIGHT. ORLANDO'S BEDROOM
ORLANDO *throws himself down into his pillows in the moonlight. Night birds cry in the distance.* ORLANDO *lies very still then slowly turns to the camera.*

ORLANDO: (*To camera*) Very interesting person.

SCENE 9: EXT. DAY. SNOWY LANDSCAPE
A procession of mourners dressed in black appears walking slowly along a path as snow falls lightly around them.
ORLANDO *is leading the procession with a long-haired dog.*
Behind the coffin bearers, three young women, CLORINDA, FAVILLA *and* EUPHROSYNE, *are walking together, their heads bowed, whispering.*

CLORINDA: (*Shaking her head*) First the Queen and now his father. It is too sad.

FAVILLA: But mourning so becomes him. One can quite see why he was the favourite.

EUPHROSYNE: My dear friends – how can you – in his time of grief . . .
> (EUPHROSYNE *is weeping gently under her black veil, whilst eyeing* ORLANDO *who walks in front of them.*
> *Cut to:*
> *Close-up of* ORLANDO, *oblivious and frozen with sadness, as his footsteps slowly crunch through the snow.*)

SCENE 10: INT. DAY. THE GREAT HOUSE

ORLANDO *stands in the Great Hall with one of his dogs, staring at an imposing ancestral portrait of his father and mother, with the Great House in the background.*
He is joined by EUPHROSYNE. *She takes his arm and together they turn to face the camera, in the same pose as his parents in the portrait.*
Cut to:
Caption:

1610
LOVE

Fade out.

SCENE 11: EXT. DAY. FROZEN RIVER THAMES

A boat is revealed trapped under the ice, a woman frozen on the deck, her lap full of red apples. There are apples all over the deck, suspended in the frozen water around her.
We hear murmured sounds of admiration for this scene. The ice has been cleared for KING JAMES. *He kneels surrounded by courtiers. They are all following his gaze, peering down with great amusement at the icy tableau.*
London Bridge towers above them. KING JAMES *turns and leads the*

group towards the Royal Enclosure. His servants skate ahead, laying silver carpets upon the ice for him to step on.

SCENE 12: EXT. DAY. ROYAL ENCLOSURE
A group of Russian Ambassadors enters the enclosure. A dark slender figure dressed in furs skates vigorously alongside them.
It is SASHA.
ORLANDO, *who is skating around in the enclosure with*
EUPHROSYNE *on his arm, catches sight of* SASHA *and stares.*
SASHA *skates effortlessly in a figure of eight, moving in vivid contrast to the women of the court who move tentatively, embarrassed and giggling with nerves, on the slippery surface.*
ORLANDO *leaves* EUPHROSYNE *and joins one of* KING JAMES's *lords in waiting.*

ORLANDO: (*In an aside*) Who is that?

EARL OF MORAY: (*Whispering*) I *believe* she is the daughter of the Muscovite Ambassador. Rather delightful . . . if that's to your taste.

ORLANDO: Whatever can you mean?

EARL OF MORAY: Oh, smearing themselves with candle wax to keep warm . . . growing beards as they get older, that kind of thing.

ORLANDO: Perhaps in this you are mistaken, Moray.

EARL OF MORAY: It was told to me on good authority by Lord Francis Vere.

ORLANDO: Has he travelled to Muscovy?

EARL OF MORAY: He knows someone who did.

ORLANDO: Ah.

> (*The Russian Ambassadors bow to* KING JAMES. SASHA *sweeps into a graceful curtsey. She looks up and her eyes flicker past* ORLANDO, *who stands staring at her, entranced.*)

SCENE 13: INT. NIGHT. ROYAL TENT (ON THE ICE)
Servants skate through the darkness in serpentine single file towards the glowing tent bearing silver trays laden with food.
A long table is set for a banquet of roast birds; the spread is decorated with ice sculptures of swans.
ORLANDO *sits next to* EUPHROSYNE. SASHA, *dressed in a deep blue velvet dress, sits opposite* ORLANDO *between* LORD FRANCIS VERE

12

and the EARL OF MORAY.

LORD FRANCIS VERE *bows to* SASHA *and announces the names of the immediate company with exaggerated enunciation.*

LORD FRANCIS VERE: The Lady Euphrosyne. The Lord Winchelsea. The Lord Orlando. The Earl of Moray.

EARL OF MORAY: Moray. (*Gesturing to his dog, cradled in his arms:*) Teasle.

LORD FRANCIS VERE: And I am Lord Francis Vere.

SASHA: Ochin liesna.

    (MORAY *and* VERE *stare uncomprehendingly at* SASHA *for a moment.*)

LORD FRANCIS VERE: Sorry?

SASHA: Enchantée.

    (*They remain baffled.*)

SASHA: Enchanted.

LORD FRANCIS VERE: Ah.

    (*The others lean back in relief now that they have understood.*)

SASHA: And my name is Alexandra Menchikova, but my father calls me Sasha.

    (ORLANDO *is watching her with intense interest.*)

ORLANDO: Enchantée.

EARL OF MORAY: (*Overly solicitous*) Here, do have some quail.

SASHA: Spasiba.

    (MORAY *exchanges quizzical glances with* VERE *and they lean back, whispering conspiratorially.*)

EARL OF MORAY: (*Whispering*) Do they have quail in Russia?

    (SASHA *leans across the table towards* ORLANDO.)

SASHA: Vous parlez français?

ORLANDO: (*Smiling*) Un peu, mais la plupart des Anglais ne peut pas, ne *veut* pas, parler d'autres langues.

    (EUPHROSYNE *watches uncomprehendingly as they speak, clearly disturbed by their complicity.*)

SASHA: Mais comment ils font pour communiquer avec les étrangers?

ORLANDO: Ils parlent anglais plus fort.

    (*Cut to:*

    The other end of the table where KING JAMES *is speaking, very loud, to the* RUSSIAN AMBASSADOR. *The* TRANSLATOR *tries to interpret but is continuously interrupted by the* KING.)

KING JAMES: (*Gesturing extravagantly*) Please tell the Ambassador that this Great Frost is the *most* severe ever to have visited these islands.

(*The* TRANSLATOR *begins to translate, but* KING JAMES *continues before he has spoken more than a few words.*)

Tell him that in Norfolk a young country woman was seen to turn visibly to *powder* and was blown away in a puff of dust in the icy blast! Most amusing.

(*The* RUSSIAN AMBASSADOR *nods politely, stroking his beard.* KING JAMES *laughs uproariously.* ORLANDO *and* SASHA *look into one anothers' eyes, smiling.*

Cut to:

Servants pulling a curtain, across the ice, of a painted trompe l'oeil scene of Neptune in an ice grotto. Behind the curtain it is revealed that the scene has been created by some shivering players as a tableau vivant.)

SCENE 14: EXT. DAY. THE ROYAL ENCLOSURE

ORLANDO *and* SASHA *are skating slowly together within the Royal Enclosure, talking animatedly.*

CLORINDA, FAVILLA *and* EUPHROSYNE *are watching them. Two* OLDER WOMEN *are whispering and gossiping. Eventually* EUPHROSYNE *rises to her feet and staggers across the ice towards* ORLANDO, *but suddenly falls awkwardly.*

ORLANDO *does not notice.*

CLORINDA *and* FAVILLA *rush to pick* EUPHROSYNE *up. The two* OLDER WOMEN *come over and help to brush her down.*

FIRST OLDER WOMAN: (*Conspiratorially*) Don't worry, my dear. This absurd affection will not last the season.

(*The other* WOMAN *raises her head and speaks pointedly and loud enough to be heard, in* ORLANDO'*s direction.*)

SECOND OLDER WOMAN: After all, she's a *foreigner.*

(SASHA *smiles at them contemptuously, shrugs and skates away from* ORLANDO *who looks angrily at the indignant* WOMEN.)

SCENE 15: EXT. NIGHT. ROYAL ENCLOSURE

KING JAMES *raises his hand for the lords and ladies to begin dancing the pavane on a dais before him.*

The Russian Ambassadors sit in a line watching the dancing with

KING JAMES.

ORLANDO *is dancing with* EUPHROSYNE *but his gaze is fixated on* SASHA, *who is skating around the dancers with grace and precision.*

EARL OF MORAY: (*In an aside as they dance*) My lord Orlando, you are in danger of becoming a fool.

(VERE *nods vigorously*. ORLANDO *shrugs*.)

Indeed, you are ruining what could be the finest career in the land. And for what?

ORLANDO: I no longer care for a career, Moray. I am only interested in love.

EARL OF MORAY: But don't you see, in courting a Cossack you are humiliating not only your fiancée, but the entire female population of this country.

VERE: Besides which, they have nothing. Why do you think they are here?

(MORAY *and* VERE *laugh derisively*.

ORLANDO *is scarcely listening, his eyes riveted on* SASHA, *who, to the scandal of those around her, is spinning and gliding about with various partners in tow.*

ORLANDO *suddenly pushes* EUPHROSYNE *aside and rushes across to* SASHA *on the ice. He kneels before her and whispers rapidly as* SASHA *skates around him in a circle*.)

ORLANDO: For your sake I would hunt wolf instead of rabbit and drink vodka instead of whisky.

SASHA: How generous!

ORLANDO: As for marriage to the good lady Euphrosyne – the thing is so palpably absurd that I scarcely give it a thought!

SASHA: How gallant!

ORLANDO: I feel as if I have been hooked through the nose and rushed through the water, painfully, yet with my own consent.

SASHA: How brave!

(SASHA *skates away.* ORLANDO *rises from his knee to be confronted by* EUPHROSYNE *who is standing, humiliated, in front of him.*)

EUPHROSYNE: My lord – have you quite forgotten that we are betrothed?

ORLANDO: My lady – I am being constantly reminded.

EUPHROSYNE: (*Bitterly*) You speak so lightly of it. You have betrayed me.

(*She throws her ring at* ORLANDO, *who lets it fall onto the ice.*)
The *treachery* of men.

(ORLANDO *stares at her as she stalks away, then turns to camera with a slightly guilty expression, which changes to one of light bravado.*)

ORLANDO: (*To camera*) It would never have worked. A man must follow his heart.

SCENE 16: EXT. DAY. FROZEN RIVER
SASHA *and* ORLANDO *are in a small sledge which is harnessed to several young men on skates. They pass through the shadows under London Bridge and hurtle on down the length of the glittering frozen river, weaving through little groups of shuffling figures going about their business in the market on the ice. One man carries a sheep. Another carries a vast bundle of twigs. Some young men race each other. A group of ragged children stands peering down into a hole in the ice where an old woman sits quietly fishing. At the edge of the crowd a troupe of acrobats is performing.*
ORLANDO *sits close to* SASHA, *watching her radiant expression as they rattle across the ice.*

SCENE 17: EXT. DAY. GREAT HOUSE

Down river, the Great House comes into view, now covered in snow and shrouded in mist.

ORLANDO *stops the sledge and stands up – pointing.*

ORLANDO: (*Proudly*) There.

SASHA: Where you live?

ORLANDO: I do.

SASHA: By yourself?

ORLANDO: Well, yes . . . at the moment.

> (ORLANDO *sits again and looks down modestly as* SASHA *stares silently at the enormous mansion.*)

SASHA: No brother? No sister?

> (ORLANDO *shakes his head then looks questioningly at* SASHA.)

ORLANDO: You, Sasha?

SASHA: If I had brothers I wouldn't be here. But my father only has me.

> *Cut to:*
>
> (*Close-up of* ORLANDO *tenderly removing* SASHA'*s glove and sensually kissing her hand.*
>
> ORLANDO *lifts his head and moves his mouth across her cheek to her mouth. They kiss slowly and sensually.*
>
> *Their kiss is interrupted by a flurry of shrieking birds and the creaking sound of footsteps walking on thin ice.*
>
> ORLANDO *slowly turns his gaze away from* SASHA *and looks into the distance.*
>
> *An old woman, bent and weary, is hobbling over the ice, an enormous bundle of brushwood across her back.*
>
> ORLANDO *pulls himself away from* SASHA'*s embrace and begins to weep.*)

ORLANDO: Nothing thicker than a knife's blade separates melancholy from happiness.

> (SASHA *stares at* ORLANDO'*s backview for a moment and then pulls him round to face her, but he continues to droop despondently.*)

SASHA: Why are you sad?

ORLANDO: Because – because – I can't bear this happiness to end.

SASHA: But we are together.

ORLANDO: Yes, now. But what about tomorrow? And the day after?

17

SASHA: Orlando, I think you suffer from a strange melancholy, which is – you suffer in advance. Look at me. Look . . .
(ORLANDO *lifts his head slowly and looks longingly at* SASHA. SASHA *gently embraces him, talking to him in a light, scolding tone.*)
You are too serious, Orlando.
(*She pauses.*)
Yet not serious enough.
(*Cut to:*
The sledge rattling across the ice in the dark blue light of dusk.)

SCENE 18: EXT. DUSK. THE RUSSIAN SHIP
ORLANDO *and* SASHA *are drawing close to the Russian ship, marooned in the ice in the mist.*
ORLANDO *helps* SASHA *up the ladder onto the deck. A sailor is waiting on the deck.*
SASHA *waves* ORLANDO *goodbye.*
ORLANDO'*s sledge is pulled onwards, but he suddenly turns and looks back towards the ship.*
ORLANDO'*s point of view: a flash of an image of* SASHA *on the deck – she is lifting her head towards the sailor, they are about to kiss . . .*
Cut to:

ORLANDO *leaps off the sledge, runs back to the boat across the ice and frantically clambers aboard.*
Confused and enraged by what he thinks he has seen, ORLANDO *lunges at the sailor, who throws him down onto the deck.*
Fade through white to:
SASHA *hovering over* ORLANDO *sinuously, cajoling him and scolding him alternately.*

SASHA: Shadows! You saw shadows!

ORLANDO: You were in his arms!

SASHA: It was illusion in light.

ORLANDO: Then what were you doing?

> (SASHA *stares at* ORLANDO.)

SASHA: (*Icily*) He was taking me across deck.

ORLANDO: But I *saw* you!

SASHA: (*Furious*) May Gods destroy me if I, family Menchikov, would lie in arms of sailor.

> (*Fade through white to:* ORLANDO *and* SASHA *standing on the deck facing each other.*)

ORLANDO: Sasha. I cannot *think* of a life without you. Stay with me. Don't ever go.

SASHA: But it's impossible.

ORLANDO: Why?

SASHA: Because when ice breaks we must go.

ORLANDO: (*Desperate*) But we're linked. Our destinies are linked. You're *mine*!

SASHA: Why?

ORLANDO: Because – I *adore* you!

> (*Fade through white to:* ORLANDO *and* SASHA *standing embracing on the prow of the ship.*)

Meet me at midnight at London Bridge. We'll fly away as free as birds! Lots of air . . . very fresh . . . (*He clasps* SASHA *to him and adds decisively:*) There, it's decided.

> (SASHA *stares out, expressionless, into the distance.*)

SCENE 19: EXT. NIGHT. THE THAMES
The sledge hurtles through the darkness on the ice.
Fireworks shoot up into the night sky. A lively, noisy crowd is gathered round a small illuminated stage raised on the ice in the distance, where a male voice (OTHELLO) can be heard declaiming.

OTHELLO: Speak of me as I am; nothing extenuate.
  Nor set down aught in malice . . .
  (*On the stage a* BOY ACTOR *dressed as a woman* [DESDEMONA],
  wearing a long fair wig, is lying on the bed; another ACTOR *with a*
  blackened face [OTHELLO] *stands nearby.*)
    . . . Then must you speak
    Of one who lov'd not wisely but too well;
    Of one not easily jealous, but, being wrought,
    Perplex'd in the extreme; of one whose hand,
    Like the base Indian, threw a pearl away
    Worth more than all his tribe;
  (ORLANDO *has joined the back of the crowd, and is watching the*
  performance admiringly.
  Cut to:
  Close-up of OTHELLO'*s agonized expression on the stage as he*
  finishes his last speech and stabs himself.)
    I kissed thee ere I killed thee. No way but this –
    Killing myself, to die upon a kiss.
  (OTHELLO *falls on the bed, kisses* DESDEMONA, *and*
  dramatically dies. The crowd roars, as ORLANDO *stares*
  transfixed, then turns to the camera.)
ORLANDO: (*Whispering, to camera*) Terrific play.

SCENE 20: EXT. NIGHT. LONDON BRIDGE
ORLANDO *is standing in the moonlight on the frozen river near London*
Bridge holding the bridles of two horses.
A child cries in the distance.
ORLANDO *pats the restless horses and then paces backwards and*
forwards through a shaft of moonlight, pausing whenever he hears a cry
or footstep.
ORLANDO: (*Muttering*) She will be here. She will.
  (*A bell strikes one. A cloud passes across the moon and suddenly*
  thunder growls and lightning flashes, illuminating ORLANDO'*s*
  anxious face.
  The clock strikes two.
  Great diamond-like drops of water are falling; at first one by one,
  gradually increasing to a torrent of rain.
  ORLANDO *stands transfixed in the downpour, finally closing his*
  eyes.

Fade out.
Cut to:
Close-up of ORLANDO *standing frozen, soaked to the skin, as a crack like a pistol shot echoes across the ice.* ORLANDO *opens his eyes and looks down.*
Cut to:
The ice cracking between ORLANDO'*s feet. The creaking, cracking sounds increase.*
Cut to:
ORLANDO *leaping from one moving ice-floe to another.*
Cut to:
ORLANDO'*s head appearing looking down over the parapet of the bridge.*
Cut to:
ORLANDO'*s point of view: great massy fragments of ice hurtle down-river beneath him.*
An ice-floe swirls past – two figures trapped on it, clinging to each other, calling desperately for help.
ORLANDO *stares out into the distance, then slowly turns and looks to the camera.*)
ORLANDO: (*Bitterly, to camera*) The treachery of women.

SCENE 21: INT. DAY. STAIRCASE AND ORLANDO'S BEDROOM
A VALET *climbs the staircase to* ORLANDO's *bedroom.*
Cut to:
Sunlight flooding in through the window of ORLANDO's *bedroom.*
ORLANDO *is asleep in bed.*
The VALET *leans over* ORLANDO *and coughs politely.*
There is no response from ORLANDO, *who continues to breathe softly.*

SCENE 22: INT. NIGHT. STAIRCASE AND ORLANDO'S
BEDROOM
Two VALETS, *the* FIRST VALET *now holding a candle, climb the
staircase.*
Cut to:
The two VALETS *standing at the bedside, gazing down at* ORLANDO's
*sleeping form. They shake his shoulder, wave their hands in front of
his face and snap their fingers, but there is no response.*

SCENE 23: INT. DAY. STAIRCASE AND ORLANDO'S BEDROOM
Three VALETS *climb the staircase.*
Cut to:
The three VALETS *standing round the bed.*
The FIRST VALET *raises his hand to bring the others in, in a chorus.*

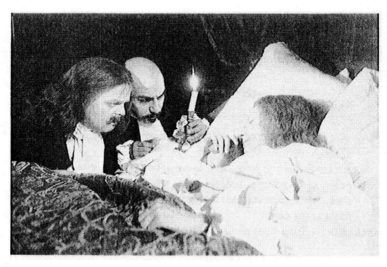

THREE VALETS: (*Shouting*) Good morning!
FIRST VALET: It is now time to *awake* –
SECOND VALET: – to such a *fine morning* –
THIRD VALET: – from such a *long, refreshing sleep.*
    (ORLANDO *remains fast asleep.*)

SCENE 24: INT. NIGHT. STAIRCASE AND ORLANDO'S
BEDROOM
A SMALL MAN *carrying a black doctor's bag hurries up the ornate
staircase behind an expressionless* BUTLER *towards a cacophony of
noise – dogs barking and a high falsetto voice singing.*
DOCTOR: Six days you say?
BUTLER: Tomorrow will be the seventh.
    (*Cut to:*
    The SINGER *is serenading the oblivious* ORLANDO.)
SINGER: '. . . This gay, this pleasing, shining, wondrous day.'
    (*The* DOCTOR *pushes his way past the* VALETS, *the* SINGER *and
    the dogs assembled in the bedroom.*
    He pulls back the covers, takes ORLANDO'S *pulse, tries to lift*
    ORLANDO'S *eyelids and then lowers his head onto* ORLANDO'S
    *chest where he listens intently. He then draws himself up and
    addresses the gathering.*)
DOCTOR: The lord Orlando is sleeping.
    (*The* VALETS *glance at each other and then look astonished as*
    ORLANDO *sits up and stretches and yawns.*)
ORLANDO: (*Sleepily*) I can find only three words to describe the
    female sex.
    (*In the ensuing silence the assembled company freezes and stares.*)
    None of which are worth expressing.
    Cut to:
    Caption:

1650
POETRY

Fade out.

SCENE 25: INT. DAY. THE LIBRARY
ORLANDO *sits in a shaft of dusty sunlight in his library, reading from
a volume of poetry.*

23

ORLANDO: (*Reading to himself*) 'When in disgrace with Fortune
and men's eyes
I all alone beweepe my out-cast state,
And trouble heaven with my bootless cries
And look upon myself and curse my fate . . .'
(*He turns to face the camera.*)
(*Softly, to camera*) Ah, poetry.

SCENE 26: EXT. DAY. GREAT HOUSE
NICK GREENE, *wearing a greasy-looking black doublet and hose,
approaches the front entrance of the Great House. He lifts the heavy
iron door knocker, then jumps back at the thunderous noise it makes.
As the door opens,* ORLANDO's *dogs rush through and jump up at*
NICK GREENE, *who cries out and tries to fend them off.* ORLANDO's
BUTLER *emerges behind the dogs.*

SCENE 27: INT. NIGHT. GREAT HALL
ORLANDO *and* NICK GREENE *are seated for dinner at either end of
the long polished table in the echoing hall. There is a tense
uncomfortable atmosphere.*
The BUTLER *fills* NICK GREENE's *wine glass and then proceeds down*

the table to ORLANDO.

NICK GREENE: (*Awkwardly*) I was thinking, sitting here, as we are, it's odd, considering how common the name of Greene is, that the Greene family came over with the Conqueror and is in fact from the highest nobility in France.

ORLANDO: (*Politely*) Oh, really?

NICK GREENE: Unfortunately, the Greenes came down in the world and we've done little more than leave our name to the Borough of Greenwich.

(*After a brief pause,* ORLANDO *leans forward earnestly.*)

ORLANDO: And now, Mr Greene, to the subject closer to my heart and yours: the sacred subject of poetry.

NICK GREENE: (*Politely*) Ah.

ORLANDO: You know – I once broke a lady's fan in my enthusiasm to find a rhyme.

NICK GREENE: (*Nodding*) Enthusiasm can be dangerous.

(NICK GREENE *is helping himself to multiple servings of soup from a huge silver tureen which he is clinging to as the* BUTLER *politely tries to wrest it away from him.*)

ORLANDO: As a youth I was often mocked for my love of poetry and solitude.

NICK GREENE: Oh. Tragic.

25

ORLANDO: And of course, Mr Greene, *your* works hold pride of place in my library.

NICK GREENE: Uh-huh.

ORLANDO: To me there is a certain glory about a man who can express in words those great emotions that others can only . . . feel.

NICK GREENE: Oh.

ORLANDO: You know, I scarcely dared to ask to make your acquaintance for I feel I can offer nothing in return . . .
(NICK GREENE *coughs, his eyes quickly roving over the lavish surroundings, then bows his head to cover his expression of irony.*)

NICK GREENE: I'm sure that any writer would be *more* than willing to accept your hospitality.

ORLANDO: (*Innocently*) Oh, do you think so?

NICK GREENE: Mmm. But if we are to speak of poetry then let us first speak of poets' *lives*. Do you know how *Hamlet* was written? Written whilst the bailiffs were pounding at Shakespeare's door. No wonder so many of his plays show the faults they do!
(NICK GREENE *looks keenly at* ORLANDO, *who nods exaggeratedly.*)

ORLANDO: Oh, I'm sure you're right.

NICK GREENE: But how can a genius work when he cannot pay the bills? And when I say *work* I mean *work*. You see – people who haven't laboured in this way don't understand that real poetry is neither easy, nor easily produced.

ORLANDO: You know, I feel that I can understand a little, Mr Greene, because I have, myself, been so rash as to attempt to write some verse . . .
(*As* ORLANDO *starts to pull a manuscript from his pocket,* NICK GREENE *jumps up, dropping his spoon with a clatter, silencing* ORLANDO.)

NICK GREENE: Did I hear a mouse's squeak?

ORLANDO: I must say, I didn't hear anything.

NICK GREENE: Doubtless then you are in good health. My own, my lord, has been so bad it's a marvel I'm still alive. I've an enlarged heart, spleen and a diseased liver. But above all there are sensations in my spine which defy description.
(*He shows* ORLANDO *his back, and then continues rapidly.*)

There's one knob about a third from the top which burns like fire! And the second from the bottom – cold as ice. Sometimes, I feel as if a thousand wax tapers were alight and that people were throwing fireworks inside my brain. And I . . . I'm so *sensitive*, I can feel a rose leaf through my mattress. In short: I am a piece of machinery so finely made and curiously put together –

(NICK GREENE *demonstrates with his filthy, ink-stained hands – which* ORLANDO *stares at fascinated.*)

– that it confounds me to think that I've only sold a hundred and fifteen copies of my poem. But it has to be said that this is largely due to what can only be described as a *conspiracy* against me.

ORLANDO: But Mr Greene – surely your work is widely admired by all the young poets, including, dare I say it –

NICK GREENE: – All the young writers will turn out any trash that will sell. It hurts me to say it – for I love literature as I love life – but the art of poetry is *dead* in England.

ORLANDO: (*Softly, after a pause*) You think so?

(NICK GREENE *reaches into his pocket and pulls out a coin, which he ripples skilfully between his fingers.*)

NICK GREENE: Of course, had I a pension of three hundred pounds a year, paid quarterly, I'd live for literature alone. I'd dedicate myself to fine writing.

(*There is a slight pause as he makes the coin appear and disappear.*)

(*Sotto voce*) But, sadly, it is necessary to have a pension to do it.

(*He executes a perfect sleight of hand with the coin, turning both palms up – empty – to* ORLANDO.)

About three hundred pounds a year. Paid quarterly.

(NICK GREENE *looks down at his fingernails then looks up at* ORLANDO's *expression which is now one of tense embarrassment.*)

SCENE 28: EXT. DAY. THE GROUNDS

ORLANDO *and* NICK GREENE *are walking together in the garden with some dogs.*

ORLANDO *suddenly, impulsively, presses a manuscript into his hands.*

27

ORLANDO: (*Gulping*) Mr Greene, I wonder, would you be so kind as to give me your opinion of *my* efforts?

(NICK GREENE *flashes a dark look at* ORLANDO.)

NICK GREENE: (*Crisply*) By all means, if I can find the *time*, for time is *money* and I must write to *eat* when not in the pursuit of *art*.

ORLANDO: (*Hurriedly*) Of course I will arrange for the small matter of the three hundred pounds –

NICK GREENE: – to be paid quarterly?

ORLANDO: As you wish.

(NICK GREENE *visibly relaxes.* ORLANDO *looks down anxiously at his manuscript.*)

NICK GREENE: (*Gushing*) My dear friend . . .

(*He looks at the title on the manuscript, holding it rather gingerly.*) 'Death . . . of a Lover'. Mmm.

(NICK GREENE *stuffs the manuscript into his bag, and hurries off, smiling.*

ORLANDO *turns to the camera, with a look of innocent triumph.*)

SCENE 29: EXT. DAY. RIVER

NICK GREENE *is seated in a small boat, clutching* ORLANDO'*s manuscript, and sniggering contemptuously. He addresses the oarsman.*

NICK GREENE: Listen to this, my friend. This is the great work of my gracious host, soon to be – congratulate me, friend – my patron!

(*He begins to read.*)

 'His heart was broken – cleft in two –
 Abandoned! Lost! What could he do?
 An end to this! he wretched cried,
 She said she loved me, but she lied!
 And so – betrayed – he fell and died!'

(NICK GREENE *is now becoming helpless with laughter.*
He puts down the manuscript for a moment to mop his eyes with a stained handkerchief, then glances back over his shoulder.
ORLANDO *stands on the riverbank in the distance, his dog by his side, waving.*
NICK GREENE *waves energetically with his handkerchief then settles back into position and in a burst of energy pulls a stub of lead from his bag and writes furiously, balancing the page on his knee,*

reading aloud as he writes.)
   'Try as he might, this gracious noble Lord
   Who lifts his pen and thinks he then can write
   Cannot – for who can pen when he is bored?
   The mind of leisure only can be trite . . .'
(*His voice continues, overlapping with* ORLANDO'*s, as the boat is
pulled rhythmically into the distance leaving a swirling eddy of
black water.*)

SCENE 30: EXT. DAY. THE GROUNDS
ORLANDO *stands next to a massive bonfire reading the rest of* NICK
GREENE'*s now printed poem aloud to himself.*
ORLANDO: (*Muttering*) '. . . This pretty knight who feebly lifts his
        sword
   To make a witless thrust against his doom
   Is foiled by what his noble birth affords –
   Dogs, dogs, more dogs and far too many rooms.
   So fortune smiles on those who own the land
   And frowns at trivia from the dabbler's hand.'
(*The* FIRST VALET *stands impassively nearby.* ORLANDO *hands
the document to him with an expression of disdain.*)
I would like you to drop this in the midst of the filthiest manure.

(*The* VALET *bows and turns to leave.*)
VALET: And Mr Greene's pension, Sir?
ORLANDO: (*Off-hand*) Pay it. Quarterly.
(ORLANDO *looks slowly, blankly, into the camera.*)

SCENE 31: EXT. DAY. THE ROYAL PALACE
ORLANDO *dressed elaborately in white and wearing a long dark
curly wig, is walking amongst the statuary with* KING WILLIAM OF
ORANGE *and* QUEEN MARY *in the palace gardens.* KING WILLIAM
*speaks with a pronounced Dutch accent, and his face wears an
expression of surprise.*
KING WILLIAM: *Abroad?*
ORLANDO: As your Ambassador, Your Majesty.
KING WILLIAM: Ambassador? I see. Once the balance of power
    has been established here in Europe, we must certainly turn
    our attention to the East.
    (*He disappears behind a heroic statue and* ORLANDO *hurries
    after him.*)
    Well, Orlando, I fear you will be quite starved for
    conversation and amusement in such a remote corner of the
    world. However, I believe they have an interest in
    horticulture . . .
    (KING WILLIAM *turns to the nearest flower bed and abruptly
    wrenches a tulip from the earth, pressing the bulb with earth
    dangling from its roots into* ORLANDO's *hands.*)
    I'd like you to bring them . . . some tulips.
    Cut to:
    Caption:

                        1700
                    POLITICS
Fade out.

SCENE 32: EXT. DAY. KHIVA (CENTRAL ASIA)
*A crowded market square, where robed and turbaned figures squat
behind great piles of eggs and pomegranates. Vendors are shouting.
The scene is chaotic, noisy and hot.*
ORLANDO *is sitting in a small swaying carriage on a camel being led
through the crowded, narrow streets. He is wearing stiff, tight,
elaborate clothing that is quite unsuitable for the heat, and is*

tulips.
Cut to:
Veiled women peering down from the small windows high in the walls.

SCENE 33: EXT. DAY. STREETS
ORLANDO, *in full ambassadorial costume, is being led through the narrow streets by a male servant in flowing robes.*
ORLANDO *is trying to maintain his dignity as passers-by stop, stare, point and then burst out laughing at* ORLANDO's *appearance.*
Some children, including a pair of small female twins, rush up and start tweaking at his red coat, sash and high-heeled boots. Finally, in desperation, ORLANDO *hands over the tulips and the twins run off shrieking with laughter.*

SCENE 34: INT. DAY. KHAN'S RESIDENCE
The male servant ushers ORLANDO *into an immense room, the ceiling supported by a forest of carved pillars, where he is greeted by a pair of male twins.*
He bows and they bow, several times, to each other.

31

ORLANDO *is led towards another pair of twins where the ritual is repeated.*

ORLANDO *is then ushered between the pillars towards his host, the* KHAN, *who is surrounded by a small retinue of twins.* ORLANDO *sweeps his hat off and bows deeply.*

KHAN: My dear Sir, please accept my hospitality. Feel that my home is your home and call upon me as you would a brother for any of your needs.

ORLANDO: You really are too kind. And I must say I am most impressed at your command of the English language – I hadn't expected . . . I mean I wasn't led to believe . . .
(There is a short awkward pause as ORLANDO *fumbles for words and the* KHAN *watches him impassively.)*

KHAN: Why are you here?

ORLANDO: I am here as a representative of His Majesty's government –

KHAN: Yes. It has been said to me that the English make a habit of collecting . . . countries.

ORLANDO: *(Protesting exaggeratedly)* Oh, we have no designs upon your sovereignty at all. No, none at all.

KHAN: You would assist us in defence against mutual enemies?
*(*ORLANDO *stares glassily, lost for words.)*

SCENE 35: INT. DAY. AMBASSADOR'S BEDROOM
ORLANDO *opens his eyes and looks slowly around him at the unfamiliar surroundings.*
His low bed is draped in layers of fine muslins. A shaft of bright golden sunlight cuts into the room from a high window.

SCENE 36: EXT. DAY. DESERT
A row of banqueting tents has been erected in the desert sand. The KHAN *stands proudly in front of it.*
A pair of male twin servants stand behind him, one bearing a gilded tray, the other a pitcher. ORLANDO *and* KHAN *face each other under the blazing sun, each ceremoniously holding small bowls.*
The KHAN *raises his bowl.*
KHAN: So Orlando, I salute your country. To England, green and pleasant land.
   (*He tosses the drink back in one gulp, then looks expectantly at* ORLANDO, *who tentatively puts the drink to his lips, gulps it down, then coughs, his eyes streaming.*
   A servant immediately re-fills his bowl. The KHAN *stands, beaming at him.* ORLANDO *realizes what is expected of him.*)
ORLANDO: And I salute *your* country. So . . . spacious and . . . so . . . warm.
   (ORLANDO *braces himself, then downs the drink once more. The* KHAN *smiles appreciatively as their bowls are swiftly re-filled.*)
KHAN: Ah yes – to the glorious sun which shines so brightly on this bountiful earth.
   (*The* KHAN *gulps down his drink – waits for* ORLANDO, *who is now sweating, but follows suit.*)
ORLANDO: Quite so.
   (ORLANDO *glazedly allows his bowl to be filled once more.*)
   (*Slightly slurred.*) Yes, yes, to . . . the beauty of nature . . .
   (ORLANDO *just manages to swallow the drink, then staggers a little.*)
KHAN: And of course to the beauty of *women*, and the joys of love.
   (*The* KHAN *raises his bowl to toast, but* ORLANDO *is looking down, silenced, swaying.*
   A row of servants watches.
   ORLANDO *stares fixedly at the sand.*)
   (*Calmly*) I see. You are here as a casualty of love, my friend.

33

(ORLANDO *sits heavily down in the sand.*)

ORLANDO: (*Muttering*) They're not like us fellows . . .

KHAN: (*Soothingly*) Women? It is said:

> 'Man should reverence
> His guardian Lord
> who created him
> From a single being
> And created, of like nature
> His mate, and from those two
> Scattered like seeds,
> Countless men and women.'

(*The* KHAN *gestures the servants away and then sits down gently beside* ORLANDO.)

So, Orlando. Let us now drink to *brotherly* love.

(ORLANDO *flings his arm dramatically round the* KHAN'*s shoulders and lifts his bowl high up towards the burning sun.*)

ORLANDO: To the *manly* virtues – Loyalty! Courage!

(ORLANDO *raises the bowl once more in a third, wordless toast. Cut to:*

A falcon swooping down towards the KHAN *and* ORLANDO *as they stand facing each other in the desert. The* KHAN *extends his arm and the falcon settles on his gloved hand.*)

SCENE 37: EXT. NIGHT. DESERT

ORLANDO *sits with the* KHAN *and his retinue around a fire which glows in the sand under the vast starry night sky.* ORLANDO *is now wearing some of the loose outer garments worn by the* KHAN *and his retinue. They are listening to a song recital, given by a group of travelling musicians. A woman sings a mournful, sinuous melody.*

ORLANDO *glances at the others, who are reclining comfortably, then tentatively lies down, pulls off his wig and with a sensuous, dreamy expression slowly closes his eyes.*

SCENE 38: INT. DAY. STEAMBATH

ORLANDO *sits wrapped in towels in the steam, his head wrapped in a turban, his feet dangling in water.*

After some confused shouts in Uzbekh, an English voice becomes clearly audible.

VOICE: Take me to your master, my good fellow.

34

(ORLANDO *looks up, startled, as the shouting continues.*)
I said, take me to your master. Does he speak English? Do you
speak English? I can assure you he will want to see me. Just let
me past, there's a good man.
(ORLANDO *sighs, lifts his feet out of the water and disappears into
the steam.*
The door is pushed open.
The voice was that of the ARCHDUKE HARRY, *who stands heavily
overdressed in dusty formal clothing, staring, rigidly, like a hare
caught in a beam of light. He is clearly startled by the vision of*
ORLANDO, *who emerges out of the steam wrapped in fine cloths;
handsome, turbaned, and barefoot.*)

ARCHDUKE: The lord Orlando?
(ORLANDO *stares at him, silent and impassive.*)
(*Flustered.*) I . . . I . . . may I present myself? I am the
Archduke Harry, emissary from Her Majesty –
(ORLANDO *remains silent.*)
(*Composing himself.*) I have come to inform you that your ten
years here as Ambassador . . . have been well appreciated by
Her Majesty, who would like to celebrate the new century by

35

raising you to the highest rank in the peerage.
ORLANDO: (*After a pause*) Ah.

SCENE 39: EXT. DAY. STREETS
ORLANDO *striding confidently through dusty, narrow streets, the*
ARCHDUKE *loping admiringly beside him and the rest of the English*
contingent following nervously behind, darting in and out of the blazing
sun.
ARCHDUKE: (*Eagerly*) There must be a party – though, of course
one must demonstrate the *gravity* of an investiture. A *large*
party – food and entertainment. But, of course, you know the
local customs. Exactly whom you should invite. Protocol.
Who's who and so forth.
(*A row of veiled women is approaching in the opposite direction,*
sweeping the street rhythmically with brooms.)

SCENE 40: INT. NIGHT. AMBASSADOR'S BEDROOM
ORLANDO *opens a trunk, pulls out his long wig and sighs, staring at it in*
the moonlight.

SCENE 41: EXT. NIGHT. COURTYARD
We hear the polite murmuring sounds of a small party.
The English contingent stand in a small stiff group in the courtyard of
ORLANDO's *Ambassadorial residence, surrounded by torchbearers.*
Servants carry trays laden with pomegranates. A huge banquet has been
laid out. Preparations have clearly been made for a much larger party
than the small number who are present.
ORLANDO *patrols the courtyard, closely followed by the* ARCHDUKE,
occasionally peering out into the darkness.
ORLANDO: Strange. Most strange.
ARCHDUKE: Perhaps they don't hold punctuality in high regard?
(ORLANDO *glances disdainfully at the* ARCHDUKE.
The English contingent mutter to each other.
Eventually, ORLANDO, *with the* ARCHDUKE *at his heels, climbs*
up to a balcony and the ceremony rather limply begins.)
(*Coughing nervously.*) As the representative of Her Majesty
Queen Anne, I am pleased and honoured to bestow the most
Noble Order of the Bath upon this loyal servant . . .
(*The English contingent applaud feebly in the echoing courtyard below.*

Cut to:
The ARCHDUKE *looking admiringly, even longingly, at*
ORLANDO.)
(*Continuing hoarsely*.) . . . for Ambassadorial services
rendered to the Crown and for the glory of, er, God.
(ORLANDO *kneels and bows his head.*
Close-up of the ARCHDUKE *sweating as he pins the Order of the*
Bath to ORLANDO's *breast, with slightly trembling fingers.*
As the ARCHDUKE *slowly and proudly lifts a ducal coronet from*
a crimson cushion, there is a sudden flurry of activity in the
courtyard below.
For a moment ORLANDO *and the* ARCHDUKE *are still and silent,*
frozen in a tableau.
Cut to:
The balcony – seen from below – where the ARCHDUKE *is still*
holding the coronet in mid-air . . . but ORLANDO *has been seized.*
Cut to:
ORLANDO *running breathlessly through the courtyard between*
twins, who drag him along, holding him by the arms, towards the
KHAN.
Figures run in all directions carrying burning torches and
swords.)

KHAN: I'm sorry to arrive in this fashion, but we must talk.
ORLANDO: But this is outrageous. I was expecting you as a guest
at my party. I didn't realize you were entertaining hostilities.
(*The* KHAN *signals to the twins, who release* ORLANDO *from*
their grip.)
KHAN: I was warned that Englishmen would be dangerous for
me, but I would like to give you an opportunity to prove this
wrong.
(*The* ARCHDUKE *appears behind* ORLANDO, *brandishing a gun.*
ORLANDO *calmly puts a hand on the* ARCHDUKE's *arm.*)
ORLANDO: Let me introduce you. This is the Archduke Harry
from England.
KHAN: Delighted. Orlando . . . our enemies are at the City Wall.
Will you help?
ORLANDO: (*Slowly*) You wish me to take arms . . .?
KHAN: Surely Orlando, you, an Englishman, are not *afraid*?
ARCHDUKE: (*Indignant*) Sir!

(ORLANDO *turns silently away. The* KHAN *stares impassively at the* ARCHDUKE, *who looks uncomfortable and confused, then turns and whispers nervously to* ORLANDO.)
My lord – despite these appalling manners – we *must* keep our interests alive in this region. What do you recommend . . .?
(ORLANDO *turns back to the* KHAN.)
ORLANDO: Harry! Distribute your arms.
ARCHDUKE: (*Low*) To these fellows? But Sir –
ORLANDO: (*Quietly*) Do as I say.
(*The* ARCHDUKE *blinks nervously, twitching, obviously fighting within himself.*
ORLANDO *and the* KHAN *stare wordlessly at each other. Then, the* KHAN *turns and strides out of the courtyard, his black coat flapping behind him.*)

SCENE 42: EXT. NIGHT. KHIVA
ORLANDO *is walking rapidly through the narrow, darkened streets, followed by the* ARCHDUKE HARRY *who is conspicuously brandishing his firearms. Some other members of the English contingent follow nervously behind.*
Figures rush chaotically in different directions.
As they reach the ramparts, where smoking fires are being lit, the KHAN *welcomes them, spreading his arms like a great black bird, and embracing* ORLANDO.
KHAN: Brother.
(*Men are piling stones on the ramparts. At a cry from a look-out they start to throw them over the edge to be met by bloodcurdling screams.*
The ARCHDUKE HARRY, *looking in his element for the first time, thrusts a gun into* ORLANDO'*s hands, then turns as a figure appears over the ramparts. The* ARCHDUKE *shoots and the man falls groaning to the ground.*
ORLANDO *runs over to him and bends over the youthful, dying man.*
The ARCHDUKE *appears at* ORLANDO'*s side.*)
ARCHDUKE: Leave him! Leave him.
ORLANDO: But this is a dying man!
ARCHDUKE: He's not a man, he is the enemy.

38

(ORLANDO *kneels, ashen-faced, looking about him in the
swirling smoke and confusion, then turning with dark questioning
eyes to the camera.*)

SCENE 43: EXT. NIGHT. KHIVA
ORLANDO *is walking away from the battle through the streets as a
stream of men rush past him in the opposite direction armed with
stones, catapults and burning torches.*

SCENE 44: INT. NIGHT. AMBASSADOR'S BEDROOM
ORLANDO *lies sleeping in a tumble of bedclothes. An* UZBEKH
DOCTOR *takes* ORLANDO's *pulse with trembling hands, as the*
MANSERVANT *stands by the bed. The* DOCTOR *then bends over and
puts his head on* ORLANDO's *chest, listening to his heartbeat (in an
echo of* ORLANDO's *sleep in Scene 24).*
The DOCTOR *and* MANSERVANT *then whisper to each other.*
DOCTOR: (*In Uzbekh*) For six days he has been like this?
MANSERVANT: (*In Uzbekh*) Tomorrow will be the seventh.

SCENE 45: INT. DAY. AMBASSADOR'S BEDROOM
*Sun streaks in through the high window. There is a slight breeze; the
muslins round the bed billow into the room.*
ORLANDO *opens his eyes and slowly takes off his long white wig,
revealing long golden red hair underneath.*
Cut to:
Close-up of ORLANDO's *hands descending into a bowl of water.*
Cut to:
Close-up of ORLANDO *splashing the water onto his face, then turning
slowly to look away.*
Cut to:
ORLANDO *is looking into a long mirror; a cool, open, curious look.*
ORLANDO *now has the body of a beautiful woman.*
Close-up as ORLANDO *looks into the camera.*
ORLANDO: Same person. No difference at all.
　　　Just a different sex.

SCENE 46: EXT. DAY. DESERT
ORLANDO *sits on a camel wearing long, black, flowing robes.*

She is at the end of a long camel train riding towards the horizon through a desert landscape in intense shimmering heat.

SCENE 47: EXT. NIGHT. GREAT HOUSE
The doors to the Great House open and the new butler and housekeeper emerge, warily, carrying lanterns in a feeble echo of Queen Elizabeth's arrival (Scene 2).
ORLANDO *approaches the house. She is wearing the same black robes as in the previous scene.*
ORLANDO: Well. Here I am again.
>(*The housekeeper and butler eye each other, then, with a habitual expression of tolerance, adapt immediately to the new situation and bow deferentially.*)

SCENE 48: INT. DAY. ORLANDO'S DRESSING ROOM
ORLANDO *is being laced into a corset by a maid.* ORLANDO *holds a mirror in her hand, occasionally wincing with pain and looking at her reflection.*
The atmosphere is sensual, private, as ORLANDO *discovers the hidden world of female clothing.*

SCENE 49: INT. DAY. GREAT HOUSE (LONG GALLERY)
ORLANDO *is walking slowly through the Long Gallery. She is
wearing a white dress with an enormously wide crinoline.
The entire interior of the gallery is covered in white drapes – tables,
chairs, beds, even paintings.*
ORLANDO's *skirts are so huge that she has trouble negotiating her
way around the furniture.
A maid crosses her path, bobbing a perfunctory curtsey.*
ORLANDO *caresses the white draped furniture as she passes, finally
coming to rest in a pool of dazzling sunlight falling through the
window.
Cut to:
Caption:*

1750
SOCIETY

Fade out.

SCENE 50: EXT. DAY. THE GREAT HOUSE
ORLANDO *is walking through the grounds past a gardener, who is
slashing at an immensely overgrown topiary shape. Around them lie
piles of leaves and branches.
Most of the topiary in front of the house has already been re-shaped
into pyramids. The influence of the East is visible; the garden has a
more extreme, architectural appearance.
The* BUTLER *approaches, carrying a pile of cards on a tray.*
BUTLER: Some more invitations, my lady.
    (ORLANDO *sifts through them, then picks one up.*)
ORLANDO: Is not this the lady famous for her literary
    gatherings?
BUTLER: Yes, Ma'am. But you could not possibly venture *there*
    alone.
ORLANDO: Why ever not?
BUTLER: *Society*, Ma'am, is full of dangerous individuals. Wits,
    and . . . poets.

SCENE 51: INT. AFTERNOON . COUNTESS'S DRAWING ROOM
*A large counter-tenor starts to sing 'Where'er You Walk', in a high,
developed voice, accompanied by harpsichord. The song continues
over the following scene.*

The COUNTESS, *wearing an extremely high wig, sits in a great armchair in the centre of a semi-circle in her overdecorated eighteenth-century city salon.*

The room is full of posturing, mannered individuals who speak and move in a fast, staccato, casually cruel way. POPE, SWIFT *and* ADDISON *are amongst the* COUNTESS's *guests, and are engaged in animated conversation, which they clearly think is extremely witty. The* ARCHDUKE HARRY *sits next to the* COUNTESS *with his back to the door.*

COUNTESS: And how *is* your leg now Mr Swift?

SWIFT: I have to tell you that the gout has left my left leg and travelled to my right.

POPE: Ah, the conversation is of legs.

SWIFT: Gout, Mr Pope.

POPE: You are an expert in this field?

SWIFT: I believe I can say I have some knowledge . . .

POPE: A little learning is a dangerous thing.

COUNTESS: Mr Pope! I must write that down at once.

POPE: (*Flashing an artificial smile*) I already have, madam.

    (*The* ARCHDUKE *laughs approvingly and leans forward in his chair confidently.*

    His speech seems slow compared to the others' quickfire repartee.)

ARCHDUKE: If taken as a science, the study of ailments can be quite *fascinating.* Indeed, I believe *science* to be more interesting than *poetry.*

POPE: (*Slightly maliciously*) Do you? Pray, sir, elaborate.

ARCHDUKE: (*Hesitates*) Well, the systematic study, *exploration,* and . . . *taming* . . . of the material world . . . is, surely, a proper occupation for a man;

    (ORLANDO *is ushered into the room. She looks strikingly beautiful, in her exaggerated clothing and immensely high wig. The* ARCHDUKE *glances at* ORLANDO, *and does a double take, then stumbles on, staring at her.*)

    compared to which the introvert art of . . . scribbling . . . is surely the occupation of . . . of . . .

POPE: – a fool?

    (*The* ARCHDUKE *blushes, transfixed by* ORLANDO. POPE, *who had been listening to the* ARCHDUKE *with a show of polite*

attention, affects a smile and then answers after a brief theatrical pause.)

POPE: Sir – I admit your general rule
    That every poet is a fool;
    But you yourself may serve to show it
    That every fool is not a poet.

COUNTESS: Mr Pope, you are pleased to be witty.
    (*There is a round of applause, led by the* COUNTESS.
    The guests re-group as tea is brought in on silver trays.
    The COUNTESS *has taken the* ARCHDUKE *aside and is now*
    busily flattering him, whispering as she pours him tea. The
    ARCHDUKE *is trembling.*)
    They are all words and no breeding, Archduke. But so
    amusing.

ARCHDUKE: (*Flustered*) Countess, forgive me, but the young lady
    who has joined us bears an *extraordinary* resemblance –

COUNTESS: The lady Orlando?

ARCHDUKE: *Orlando?*

COUNTESS: And we're so proud of you, Harry. The Order of the
    Bath. Marvellous. Cream?
    (ORLANDO, *who has been sitting alone playing with her fan and*
    appears to be confused about what is expected of her, is ushered
    by ADDISON *into the poets' circle.*)

ADDISON: Well, how pleasant it is idly to sip tea in the presence of
    a gracious lady.

SWIFT: (*Smiling*) Indeed, Mr Addison, as our good friend Dr
    Johnson says, 'Every man is, or desires to be, an idler.'
    (*The* COUNTESS *calls out across the room.*)

COUNTESS: Perhaps not every woman, Mr Swift.

SWIFT: Women have no desires, only affectations.
    (*The* COUNTESS *titters appreciatively.*)

POPE: Indeed, women are but children of a larger growth.
    (ORLANDO *freezes, staring at* POPE.)

ADDISON: Ah – but *I* consider woman as a beautiful, romantic
    animal who should be adorned in furs and feathers, pearls
    and diamonds.
    (*He turns and bows to* ORLANDO.)
    (*Turning to* POPE.) Apart from my wife, of course, who will
    insist on attempting to learn *Greek*, which is so very

45

unbecoming I can hardly tolerate her company at the
breakfast table. Why *do* they do it?

POPE: Oh, every woman is *at best* a contradiction. And frankly,
most women have no characters at all.

ADDISON: Present company excepted, of course.

(*The men laugh, bowing lightly towards* ORLANDO, *who
remains quiet and still, but looks increasingly flushed.*)

POPE: Oh! The lady is aflame. And silent. Perfect!

(ORLANDO *slowly puts down her teacup.*)

ORLANDO: Gentlemen. I find it strange . . . You are poets, each
one of you, and speak of your muse in the feminine, and yet
you appear to feel neither tenderness nor respect towards
your wives nor towards females in general.

(*There is a sudden silence in the salon. The* COUNTESS *freezes,
listening intently. The* ARCHDUKE *is gazing at* ORLANDO,
astonished.)

ADDISON: (*With a tight-lipped smile*) Madam, I have only the
highest regard and purest respect for females.

ORLANDO: I find no evidence of that sentiment in your
conversation.

POPE: Conversation is a place where one plays with *ideas*, my dear
lady, though one forges them quite alone.

SWIFT: Quite so.

ADDISON: (*Muttering*) Quite, quite.

POPE: The intellect is a *solitary* place and therefore quite
unsuitable a terrain for females who must discover their
natures through the guidance of a father or husband.

ORLANDO: And if she has neither?

POPE: Then, however charming she may be, my dear lady, she is
lost.

(*After a pause,* ORLANDO *turns and looks silently into the
camera.*)

SCENE 52: EXT. DAY. THE GREAT HOUSE

ORLANDO *is walking angrily up the path towards the entrance to the
house.* HARRY *is trotting by her side, and has clearly been talking for
some time.*

HARRY: None of us knew what had happened. It is extraordinary!
And to think we could have been so *charmingly* misled.

46

(ORLANDO *sighs with exasperation, lifts her petticoats and walks once more with her familiar 'male' stride between the topiary pyramids.*

The BUTLER *hurries anxiously towards* ORLANDO, *with two* OFFICIAL-LOOKING MEN *following close behind her into the garden.*

They nudge each other as ORLANDO *stops and one of them steps forward.*)

FIRST OFFICIAL: The *Lady* Orlando?

ORLANDO: (*Bowing slightly*) The same.

    (*The* SECOND OFFICIAL *steps forward, hovering slightly behind the first.*)

FIRST OFFICIAL: We wish to inform you, er, Madam, that you are a party to several major law suits that have been preferred against you concerning the property.

SECOND OFFICIAL: (*Smirking*) The family seat.

ORLANDO: Pray continue.

    (*The* FIRST OFFICIAL *coughs and unfurls a document.*)

FIRST OFFICIAL: (*Sotto voce*) One. You are legally dead and therefore cannot hold any property whatsoever.

ORLANDO: Ah. Fine.

FIRST OFFICIAL: Two. You are now female –

SECOND OFFICIAL: (*Gleefully*) – which amounts to much the same thing.

    (ORLANDO *listens glazedly.*)

FIRST OFFICIAL: (*Restraining the* SECOND OFFICIAL) Pending the legal judgment, however, you have the law's permission to reside in the property in a state of incognito –

SECOND OFFICIAL: – or incognit*a*, as the case may be . . .

    (*The* ARCHDUKE HARRY *suddenly lunges for* ORLANDO'*s hand.*)

ORLANDO: Harry!

ARCHDUKE: There is only one solution in your current predicament.

ORLANDO: Indeed?

ARCHDUKE: I can offer you a house to rival your own!

ORLANDO: I don't quite understand.

    (*The* ARCHDUKE *goes down on one knee.*)

ARCHDUKE: (*Laughing nervously*) I confess! Orlando – to me – you

47

48

were, and always will be – whether male *or* female – the pink, the
   pearl and the perfection of your sex. I am offering you my hand.
   (*The* OFFICIALS *bow and leave, coughing and embarrassed.*)
ORLANDO: Oh Archduke! That's very kind of you – yes – but I
   cannot accept.
ARCHDUKE: But I . . . I . . . *am England*. And you are *mine*!
ORLANDO: I see – On what grounds?
ARCHDUKE: (*Despairingly*) That I *adore* you!
ORLANDO: And this means that I belong to you?
   (ORLANDO *and the* ARCHDUKE *stare at each other.*)
ARCHDUKE: You are refusing me?
ORLANDO: I am. I'm sorry.
   (*The* ARCHDUKE *stumbles to his feet, looking incredulous and
   hurt.*)
ARCHDUKE: But Orlando, with your history – quite frankly – who
   else would have you? Do you realize what you are turning
   down? With your . . . ambiguous sexuality – which I am
   prepared to tolerate – this is your last chance of respectability.
ORLANDO: (*Panting*) I can't breathe –
ARCHDUKE: – you will die a spinster. Dispossessed and alone.
   (ORLANDO *turns on her heel, lifts her voluminous skirts and
   indignantly strides away across the garden.*
   Cut to:
   ORLANDO *as she pauses at the entrance to a maze and looks back
   to the camera.*)
ORLANDO: (*To camera*) Spinster!
   (ORLANDO *disappears into the maze, then reappears for a moment
   to add:*)
   (*To camera*) Alone!

SCENE 53: EXT. DAY. THE MAZE
As ORLANDO *walks furiously through the maze, turning and twisting
between the high clipped hedges, the pale sunlight is gradually replaced
by the damp swirling mist of the Victorian era.*
ORLANDO'*s clothing also changes – from her pale decorated eighteenth-
century clothes and wig, to a dark-green Victorian jacket and crinoline.*

SCENE 54: EXT. DAY. MOORLAND
The landscape is wild, devastated and windswept.

ORLANDO *appears, wild-eyed out of the mist.*
She lifts her heavy skirts and runs as the camera swoops, bird-like,
behind her to the sound of heavily romantic music.
ORLANDO *suddenly trips and falls.*
She lies stunned, prostrate, face down with arms outstretched, like a
nun offering herself as a bride to Christ.
ORLANDO: (*Panting*) Nature, nature. I am your bride! Take me!
(ORLANDO *is closing her eyes when she hears something, lifts*
her head and looks into the distance.)
Cut to:
Caption:

1850
SEX

Fade out.
(ORLANDO *looks up as a horse and rider* [SHELMERDINE]
gallop towards her out of the mist.
The horse rears up, startled by ORLANDO's *prostrate figure.*
SHELMERDINE *is flung to the ground, and lies spreadeagled in*
front of ORLANDO.
ORLANDO *looks questioningly into the camera.*
SHELMERDINE *slowly raises his head. He is dark-haired, wild-*
looking and extremely handsome.)

SHELMERDINE: You're hurt, Ma'am.

ORLANDO: I'm dead, sir!

> (SHELMERDINE *pauses, carefully scrutinizing* ORLANDO's *expression.*)

SHELMERDINE: (*Lightly*) Dead. That's serious. Can I help?

ORLANDO: Will you marry me?

SHELMERDINE: Ma'am, I would gladly – but –

> (SHELMERDINE *winces in pain as he tries to move.* ORLANDO *looks startled.*)

> I fear my ankle is twisted.

SCENE 55: EXT. DAY. ENGLISH LANDSCAPE

ORLANDO *and* SHELMERDINE *are galloping through the misty landscape;* ORLANDO *is holding the reins while* SHELMERDINE *perches behind her, his arms around her waist.*

Suddenly there is a shrieking whistle and the thundering sound of an approaching steam train.

The scene is enveloped in a cloud of steam.

ORLANDO *just manages to keep the horse under control.*

ORLANDO: What's that?

SHELMERDINE: The future!

SCENE 56: INT. EVENING. GREAT HALL

ORLANDO *is carrying a bowl of steaming milk towards* SHELMERDINE, *who now lies on a chaise longue by the fire, his ankle propped up by pillows.*

The Great Hall now has a Victorian look to it – heavy dark drapes at the windows, some gaslight fixtures, a baize cloth on the table . . .

ORLANDO *solicitously offers* SHELMERDINE *the bowl of hot milk.*

ORLANDO: Some milk? My God, I don't yet know your name, Sir. How strange – I feel as though I know everything about you.

SHELMERDINE: (*Inclining his head*) When like meets like . . . my name is Shelmerdine, Ma'am.

ORLANDO: Orlando. So. It only remains to fill in such unimportant details as –

SHELMERDINE: – what we do and so on?

ORLANDO: Well, you can see for yourself what I *was*.

SHELMERDINE: *Was*?

(ORLANDO *gestures at the Hall with its ancestral portraits, then pours a kettle of steaming water into a bowl by the fire. She gently lowers* SHELMERDINE's *foot into the water. The firelight and the water send reflections rippling across* ORLANDO's *face, as she gazes into* SHELMERDINE's *eyes.*)

ORLANDO: You see – I am about to lose everything –

SHELMERDINE: – then you can come with me.

ORLANDO: Where are you going?

SHELMERDINE: Back to America – when the wind changes to the south-west.

ORLANDO: America? I've been abroad – but East –

SHELMERDINE: Then you know as well as I how good it is to travel. Like a free spirit – unfettered by position or possession.

ORLANDO: Unfettered? Are you an . . . adventurer . . . by profession?

SHELMERDINE: My profession, if you can call it that, is the pursuit of liberty . . .

(SHELMERDINE *leans back sensuously into the cushions.* ORLANDO *looks down again, splashing water over* SHELMERDINE's *foot.*)

(*Murmuring*) 'Like the bright shade of some immortal dream

Which walks, when tempest sleeps . . .'

(ORLANDO *has stopped moving*)

ORLANDO: '. . . The wave of life's dark stream.'

SHELMERDINE: (*Low*) You do not really want a husband.

ORLANDO: (*Ignoring him*) I suppose your journeys to be hazardous at times?

SHELMERDINE: I think you want . . . a lover.

ORLANDO: You have fought, in battles, like a man?

SHELMERDINE: I have fought.

ORLANDO: Blood?

SHELMERDINE: If necessary, yes. Freedom must be *taken*. Freedom must be *won*.

(ORLANDO *stares at* SHELMERDINE. *He smiles back at her.*)

ORLANDO: (*Tentatively*) If I were a man . . .

SHELMERDINE: You?

ORLANDO: I might choose *not* to risk my life for an uncertain cause. I might think that freedom won by death was not worth having. In fact –

SHELMERDINE: (*Shrugging*) – you might choose not to be a *real man* at all . . . say if I was a woman.

ORLANDO: You?

SHELMERDINE: I might choose not to sacrifice my life caring for my children, nor my children's children. Nor to drown anonymously in the milk of female kindness. But instead – say – to go abroad. Would I then be –

(ORLANDO *and* SHELMERDINE *look at each other, and both smile in recognition.*)

ORLANDO: – a real woman?

(ORLANDO *slowly rises and draws* SHELMERDINE *into her arms. She turns radiantly to the camera, clasping* SHELMERDINE *to her breast.*)

(*To camera*) I think I'm going to faint. I've never felt better in my life.

SCENE 57: INT. NIGHT. ORLANDO'S BEDROOM

ORLANDO *and* SHELMERDINE *are lying luxuriantly amongst the immense feather pillows in her bed.*

ORLANDO *lies above* SHELMERDINE *and caresses him tentatively and joyfully, as if touching someone for the first time.*

SHELMERDINE *remains resolutely passive.*

Cut to:

ORLANDO *sitting in the bed looking at* SHELMERDINE *who lies on his back, looking vulnerable and open, gazing at her.*

Cut to:

As the erotic tension builds, the camera moves in closer and closer. The contours of their bodies start to resemble landscapes: hills and furrows, light and shade, skin and hair.

Finally, the camera comes to rest on ORLANDO's *unblinking eye.*

SCENE 58: INT. DAY. ORLANDO'S BEDROOM

The crumpled sheets are dappled with sunlight. SHELMERDINE *has curled around* ORLANDO, *murmuring into her ear, like a lullaby.*

SHELMERDINE: 'I arise from dreams of thee

In the first sweet sleep of night

When the winds are breathing low

54

And the stars are shining bright . . .'
(ORLANDO *stirs and opens her eyes.*)

ORLANDO: (*Sleepily*) But it is day.

SHELMERDINE: Days and nights have mingled in your sweet
embrace, Orlando.
(*We hear a knock at the door. After a pause the knocking
increases in urgency. Eventually* ORLANDO *reluctantly
answers.*)

ORLANDO: Who's there?

BUTLER: (*Outside*) Excuse me, m'lady, there are two officers
outside with a warrant from the Queen.

ORLANDO: The Queen?

BUTLER: (*Outside*) Victoria, Ma'am. The gentlemen say they
must speak to you in person.
(ORLANDO'*s face falls.*)

ORLANDO: Oh. I had almost forgotten . . .

SCENE 59: EXT. DAY. GREAT HOUSE
The two OFFICERS *are waiting at the door to the house. The front of
the house is now entirely covered in greenery – moss, ivy and grass;
the front door is almost obscured by hanging fronds.
It is raining.*

The BUTLER *opens the door for* ORLANDO *and* SHELMERDINE.

BUTLER: Her Ladyship.

> (*The* OFFICERS *formally hand* ORLANDO *a legal document.*
> ORLANDO *reads it, running her finger over the pages, murmuring and then reading certain passages aloud.*)

ORLANDO: The lawsuits are settled. My sex is pronounced indisputably, and beyond the shadow of a doubt . . . female. Therefore, heirs male of my body . . .

> (ORLANDO *pauses.*)

Well, the rest can be taken as read. I lose everything unless I have a son.

> (ORLANDO *turns and looks boldly at the* OFFICERS. *They are looking down, embarrassed, at their feet. She then takes the pen and signs the document with a flourish.*
>
> *The* OFFICERS *take the document, bow, and retreat through the house.*
>
> ORLANDO *walks into the courtyard followed by* SHELMERDINE. *Greenery now covers everything. Choking ivy, weeds, and ferns cover the stone urns, steps and walls.*
>
> *Some of the topiary has been clipped into Victorian teacup shapes.*)

SHELMERDINE: So – you are free.

ORLANDO: (*Lightly*) I think the spirit of this century has finally taken me and broken me.

SHELMERDINE: (*Tenderly*) That would be sad if it were true, but it is not. Come with me!

ORLANDO: I cannot. I can't just follow you.

SHELMERDINE: You can stay and stagnate in the past or leave and live for the future! The choice is yours.

ORLANDO: As a *man* one has choices, Shelmerdine.

SHELMERDINE: Orlando, you can do whatever you want.

(ORLANDO *turns and looks directly at* SHELMERDINE.)

ORLANDO: Would you like to have a child with me?

SHELMERDINE: So that you can keep your house?

ORLANDO: No, not for the house, Shelmerdine. Perhaps for love.

(SHELMERDINE *turns and walks away, gesturing grandly*.)

SHELMERDINE: These are the times that try men's souls. My love is for mankind, I must fight for liberty. I must fight for a —

ORLANDO: (*Interrupting*) — future? This future of yours, Shelmerdine, when is it going to begin? Today? Or is it always tomorrow?

(SHELMERDINE *smiles*.)

SHELMERDINE: (*Tenderly*) Touché, Orlando.
> (*A swirl of leaves suddenly blows across their path. They look at each other.*)

ORLANDO: The wind!

SHELMERDINE: The wind!

ORLANDO: The south-west wind!
> (*After a pause they fall into each others' arms and kiss passionately.*
>
> *Cut to:*
>
> ORLANDO *holding the stirrup of* SHELMERDINE'*s horse.*
> SHELMERDINE *mounts the horse in one bound. The horse leaps forward, tossing its mane.*)

Goodbye, Shelmerdine! Good luck!

SHELMERDINE: Orlando!
> (*The horse rears up and then* SHELMERDINE *gallops away, waving as he disappears into the mist.*
>
> ORLANDO *smiles, gazing into the distance.*
>
> *Then the rain starts – heavy, lashing rain.*
>
> ORLANDO *stands immobile in the rain – then finally, with a sigh, closes her eyes.*
>
> *Fade out.*
>
> *Cut to:*
>
> *The rain has stopped.* ORLANDO *opens her eyes and slowly and calmly turns to look at the camera. Her expression gradually changes as she hears the growing roar of an aeroplane passing directly overhead. She looks up.*
>
> *We hear an explosion.*)

SCENE 60: EXT. NIGHT. WASTELAND

ORLANDO *is running across a dark expanse of devastated wasteland, dressed now in clothes from the 1940s.*

Explosions in the distance and flares occasionally illuminate the wrecked landscape – bare except for some abandoned artillery pieces and coils of barbed wire.

In a particularly violent explosion ORLANDO *trips and falls. We see that she is pregnant.*

Cut to:

Close-up of ORLANDO *lying in the mud, as the sound of bullets and bombs continue to whistle overhead. She gets up, clutches her belly,*

and stumbles on.
Cut to:
ORLANDO *walking on through the battlefield into a misty dawn.*
Cut to:
Caption:

BIRTH

Fade out.

SCENE 61: INT. DAY. OFFICE
A manuscript thumps down onto a desk.
ORLANDO *is sitting on an immense leather sofa in an ultra-modern chrome and glass office.*
A MALE EXECUTIVE PUBLISHER *(who looks like an extremely smart, sharp-suited version of* NICK GREENE*) sits behind a huge black desk with* ORLANDO'*s rather battered manuscript in front of him.*
PUBLISHER: It's really very good. Written from the heart. I
   think it will sell.
   (There is a pause as ORLANDO *listens impassively.)*
   Providing you re-write a little. You know, develop the love
   interest and give it a happy ending.
   (He fingers the stained manuscript rather gingerly.)

59

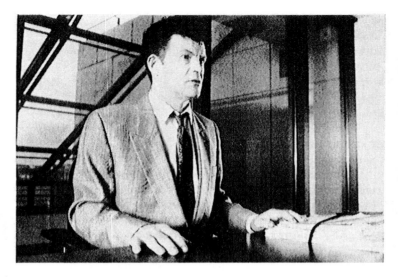

By the way, how long did this draft take you . . .?
(ORLANDO *looks knowingly to the camera.*)

SCENE 62: EXT. DAY. MODERN STREET (DOCKLANDS)
Close-up of ORLANDO's *foot starting a motorbike.*

Cut to:
Medium shot of ORLANDO *riding a motorbike with a side-car. In the side-car sits a young girl – her* DAUGHTER. *They are both wearing goggles and flying helmets, and are clearly enjoying the ride. The modern urban landscape of London's Docklands blurs behind them.*

SCENE 63: EXT. DAY. GREAT HOUSE
ORLANDO *arrives at the Great House on her bike with her daughter in the side-car.*
The façade, lawn, and topiary pyramids are entirely covered in white plastic, which is flapping and shining in the wind and sunlight. They come to a halt, and ORLANDO *follows her* DAUGHTER *as she dashes about joyfully amongst the plastic forms.*
ORLANDO: (*Voiceover*) She – for there can be no doubt about her sex – is visiting the house she finally lost for the first time in over a hundred years. She does still have certain natural advantages, of course. She is tall and slim, with the slightly androgynous appearance that many females of the time aspire to . . .

SCENE 64: INT. DAY. GREAT HALL
ORLANDO's *voiceover continues as: a sudden flash illuminates the Great Hall. Tourists are pointing and taking photographs.*
Cut to:
Reverse angle: The tourists are photographing a portrait of ORLANDO *as a young man.*
ORLANDO *stands holding her* DAUGHTER, *looking at the portrait.*
ORLANDO: (*Voiceover continues*) . . . Then, her upbringing. She's lived for four hundred years and hardly aged a day. And, because this is England, everyone pretends not to notice. But she has changed . . .

SCENE 65: EXT. DAY. OAK TREE
ORLANDO's *voiceover continues over:*
A wild hand-held point of view video image – running through long grass.
ORLANDO: (*Voiceover*) She's no longer trapped by destiny. And ever since she let go of the past, she found her life was beginning.

(Cut to:

ORLANDO's DAUGHTER *dashing about with a small video camera – it is her point of view we are watching. Meanwhile,* ORLANDO *is sitting under the oak tree in much the same position as in Scene I, watching her daughter.*
Cut to:
Video shot: ORLANDO's DAUGHTER's *point of view, rushing towards* ORLANDO *through the grass.*
ORLANDO *is crying but looks radiant. She is looking up into the sky.)*

DAUGHTER: Why are you sad?

ORLANDO: I'm not. I'm happy. Look. Look up there.

(ORLANDO's DAUGHTER *turns her camera chaotically to the sky. There, hovering in the sky, is the* FALSETTO *who sang for* QUEEN ELIZABETH *as she made her stately passage along the river four hundred years previously.*
He is dressed in gold, has wings, and is singing in his high voice to ORLANDO *as he flies in the sky above:)*

ANGEL: I am coming! I am coming!
I am coming through!
Coming across the divide to you
In this moment of unity
I'm feeling only an ecstasy
To be here, to be now
At last I am free –
Yes – at last, at last
To be free of the past
And of a future that beckons me.

I am coming! I am coming!
Here I am!
Neither a woman nor a man –
We are joined, we are one
With a human face
We are joined, we are one
With a human face
I am on earth
And I am in outer space
I'm being born and I am dying.

(ORLANDO *slowly looks into the camera – an open, radiant, steady gaze.*
We have arrived in the present moment.
The song continues over the end credits.)

Orlando was first shown as part of the official Competition at the Venice Film Festival in September 1992.

Front titles

Adventure Pictures
presents

a co-production with
Lenfilm
Mikado Film
Rio
Sigma Filmproductions

with the participation of
British Screen

Co-producers
Roberto Cicutto
Jean Gontier
Matthijs Van Heijningen
Luigi Musini
Vitaly Sobolev

a film by
Sally Potter

based on the book by
Virginia Woolf

Orlando

Tilda Swinton
Billy Zane
Lothaire Bluteau
John Wood
Charlotte Valandry
Heathcote Williams
and
Quentin Crisp

with
Peter Eyre
Thom Hoffman
Kathryn Hunter
Ned Sherrin
Jimmy Somerville
Dudley Sutton

Casting	Irene Lamb
Costume Design	Sandy Powell
Additional Costume Design	Dien Van Straalen
Production Design	Ben Van Os
	Jan Roelfs
Music Supervisor	Bob Last
Editor	Herve Schneid
Director of Photography	Alexei Rodionov
Produced by	Christopher Sheppard
Written and directed by	Sally Potter

End credits

Cast (in order of appearance)

ORLANDO	Tilda Swinton
QUEEN ELIZABETH I	Quentin Crisp
SINGER	Jimmy Somerville
ORLANDO'S FATHER	John Bott
ORLANDO'S MOTHER	Elaine Banham
CLORINDA	Anna Farnworth
FAVILLA	Sara Mair-Thomas
EUPHROSYNE	Anna Healy
KING JAMES I	Dudley Sutton
EARL OF MORAY	Simon Russell Beale
LORD FRANCIS VERE	Matthew Sim
TRANSLATOR	Jerome Willis
RUSSIAN AMBASSADOR	Victor Stepanov
SASHA	Charlotte Valandrey
FIRST WOMAN	Mary MacLeod
SECOND WOMAN	Barbara Hicks
RUSSIAN SAILOR	Alexander Medvedev

OTHELLO	Toby Stephens
DESDEMONA	Oleg Pogodin
FIRST VALET	George Yiasoumi
SECOND VALET	Toby Jones
THIRD VALET	Robert Demeger
BUTLER	Lol Coxhill
DOCTOR	Thom Osborn
SINGING VALET	Giles Taylor
NICK GREENE	Heathcote Williams
KING WILLIAM OF ORANGE	Thom Hoffman
QUEEN MARY	Sarah Crowden
THE KHAN	Lothaire Bluteau
ARCHDUKE HARRY	John Wood
SECOND BUTLER	Hugh Munro
HARPSICHORDIST	Peter Hayward
COUNTER TENOR	Andrew Watts
COUNTESS	Kathryn Hunter
MR SWIFT	Roger Hammond
MR POPE	Peter Eyre
MR ADDISON	Ned Sherrin
YOUNG MAN	Cyril Lecomte
YOUNG WOMAN	Olivia Lancelot
FIRST OFFICIAL	John Grillo
SECOND OFFICIAL	Martin Wimbush
SHELMERDINE	Billy Zane
THIRD BUTLER	Terence Soall
PUBLISHER	Heathcote Williams
ORLANDO'S DAUGHTER	Jessica Swinton
ANGEL	Jimmy Somerville

made with the assistance of
The European Co-production Fund (UK)

developed with the support of
The European Script Fund
an initiative of the media programme of the European Community
and
The National Film Development Fund
London, England

67

Production Executives	Anna Vronskaya
	Linda Bruce
Line Producer	Laurie Borg
Associate Producers	Lynn Hanke
	Richard Salmon
	Martine Kelly
First Assistant Directors	Michael Zimbrich
	Chris Newman
Second Assistant Director	Simon Moseley
Third Assistant Director	Christian McWilliams
Story Editor	Walter Donohue
Script Supervisor	Penny Eyles
Director's Assistant	Renny Bartlett
Production Coordinator	Jonathan Finn
Location Manager	Tony Clarkson
Production Associate (Russia)	Zamir Gotta
Production Coordinator (Russia)	Harriet Earle
Production Supervisor (Holland)	Guurtje Buddenberg
Production Assistant (Holland)	Annemieke Heep
Producer's Assistant	Roanne Moore
Production Runners	Simon Fraser
	James Norton
Focus Pullers	Lucy Bristow
	Boris Galper
	Mike Robinson
Clapper Loaders	Anatoly Mannanikov
	Grant Branton
Grip	Richard Broome
Sound Recordist	Jean-Louis Ducarme
Boom Operator	Samuel Cohen
Set Designer (Russia)	Christopher Hobbs
Art Directors	Michael Buchanan
	Michael Howells
Production Buyer	Totty Whately
Set Dressers	Constance de Vos
	Floris Vos
Assistant Art Directors	Ank van Straalen
	Sam Riley
Art Department Coordinators	Eljo Embregts
	Han Ing Lim
Art Department Assistants	Drogo Michie
	Menno Verduin

Prop Makers	Linda Termars
	Helen Huisman
Scenic Artist	Todd van Hulzen
Art Department Graphics	Joshua Meath Baker
Art Department Trainee	Joost Bongers
Costume Supervisor	Paul Minter
Wardrobe Supervisor	Clare Spragge
Wardrobe Assistants	Nigel Egerton
	Tim Guthrie
	Marie Therese Jacobse
Wardrobe Trainee	Michael Weldon
Costume Makers	John Krausa
	Brian Collings
	Doreen Brown
	Pam Downe
	Maria Llyjfors
	Carmel Kelly
	Peter Lewis
Wardrobe Buyer	Paula Dumont
Jewellery	Simon Costin
Fabric Dyer & Printer	Mathilde Sandberg
Additional Costume Makers	Mark Bauman
	Deborah Bulleid
	Annie Symons
	Keith Collins
	Sandra Wallas
	Clare Muller
	Alfie McHugh
	Stephen Brimson Lewis
	Cath Pater-Llancuki
Millinery	Juliette Monro
	Vanessa Monro
	Kate Slee
Costumiers	Gordon Harmer
	Caroline Hume
Make-up Supervisor	Morag Ross
Make-up Assistant	Miri Ben Shlomo
Hairdressing Supervisor	Jan Archibald
Assistant Hairdresser	Sian Grigg
Wigs by	London Wigs
Gaffer	Ted Read
Best Boy	Barry Read

Electrician	Steve Read
Generator Operator	Bob Gomme
Construction Manager	Wilbert van Dorp
Standby Carpenter	Steve Challenor
Standby Rigger	Tom Lowen
Construction Team	Maarten Piersma
	Dory van Noort
	Lidewij Kapteyn
	Rob Duiker
	Elmer Jacobs
	Colin Yair Lewis
	Dennis Los
Head Setpainter	Ben Zuidwijk
Setpainter	John Rawsthorn
Trainee	Esther van Wijk
Choreographer	Jacky Lansley
Stunt Cordinator	Steve Dent
Special Effects Technician	Paul Corbould
Stand-ins	Annie Livings
	Alan Meacham
Unit Driver	Jeffrey Oldman
Props Truck Driver	Brian's Props & Locations
Artists' Cars	Focus Transport Services
Transport	GT Transport
Freight Agent (UK)	Dynamic International
Freight Agent (Russia)	Armadillo
Catering (Russia)	Capital Catering
Catering (UK)	Location Caterers
Motorolas	Wavevend

Additional production crew (St Petersburg)

Production Manager	Yuri Glotov
Production Coordinator	Natalia Tokarskikh
Production Assistants	Gabrielle Scott
	Yevgeni Reshetnikov
	Vladimir Yegorov
	Katya Nikolayeva
	Vladimir Malkin

Translators	Marat Husainov
	Lubava Popova
	Andrei Peshehodov
	Masha Averbach
	Vitaly Yerenkov
	Valera Katsuba
	Marina Maidanuk
	Tomaz Lasica
	Vera Levitskaya
	Kelly Richdale
	Inna Musina
Casting Director	Liubov Vlasenko
Casting Assistant	Nikita Mikhailov
First Assistant Director	Yuri Vertlib
Third Assistant Directors	Sasha Yurchikov
	Gabrielle Vorobiev
Camera Department Supervisor	Vadim Grammatikov
Grips	Andrei Zdorov
	Vladimir Kudriatsev
Gaffer	Sergei Vinogradov
Art Director	Stanislav Romanovsky
Assistant Art Directors	Vasily Reva
	Valeria Volynskaya
Props	Dmitri Masloboyev
Props Assistant	Irina Bylinskaya
Wardrobe Mistress	Ludmila Romanovskaya
Wardrobe Assistant	Irina Kotova
Costume Maker	Tatiana Morozova
Make-up Artist	Tamara Fried
Make-up Assistants	Natalia Gorina
	Marina Lebedeva
	Irina Braninova
Special Effects Directors	Yuri Borovkov
	Viktor Okovitey
Stunt Coordinator	Oleg Vasilug
Pyrotechnics	Sergei Maslikov
Carpenters	Mikhail Azhishev
	Yuri Tomachayev
Labourers	Vladimir Grieshnikov
	Piotr Tabus
	Sergei Andreyev
	Sergei Tribunski.

Mechanic	Sergei Lateshevsky
Unit Drivers	Anatoly Kuharchik
	Igor Shishko
	Ira Pleshakova
	Viktor Shevyakov
Accountant	Ludmila Sadovskaya
Cashier	Alla Blochina

Additional production crew (Uzbekhistan)

Head of Production	Radjabov Muhamedjan
Deputy Head of Production	Feodor Tumenev
Administrators	Jskander Jsmatov
	Asror Sharipov
	Anna Masimova
Translator	Walter Krakovtsev
First Assistant Director	Rikhsivoj Abduvakhidov
Grips	Abduvakhid Akhmedkhanov
	Tolrukh Zijathanov
Art Director	Igor Gulyenko
Set Dressers	Rashid Sharafutdinov
	Feodor Shoakhmedov
	R Majsoyutov
Props	Otkham Mizzaev
	Bahodiz Atbasarov
Costume Supervisor	Zibo Nassirova
Wardrobe Assistants	Larisa Sherbina
	Almira Yambaeva
Gaffer	Rikhsivoj Abduvakhidov
Best Boy	Khasan Usmanov
Electricians	Aziz Djakhangirov
	Rihsivoj Parpier
	Asror Umarov
	Mikhail Junusov
Pyrotechnics	Nikolaj Borisov
	Alexandr Pantushin
Transport Manager	Gajrat Sobirov
Accountant	Vera Kostovatova
Cashier	Valentina Tugova
First Assistant Editor	Nick Moore
Second Assistant Editor	Michael Trent
Supervising Sound Editor	Kant Pan

Dialogue Editor	Martin Evans
Assistant Sound Editor	Victoria Boydell
Foley	Martyn Robinson
Re-recording Mixer	Robin O'Donoghue
Assistant Re-recording Mixer	Dominic Lester
Foley Artists	Dianne Greaves
	Jack Stew
	Pauline Bennion
Post-Production Facilities	Goldcrest
Re-recording	Twickenham Film Studios
ADR Recorded at	Mayflower Film Recording
Production Lawyer	Diane Gelon
Legal Consultant	Julian Dickens, Simon Olswang & Co
Production Accountant	Richard Hyland
Assistant Accountant	Stella Hyland
Cashier (Holland)	Fred Homan
Stills Photographer	Liam Longman
Publicity	Corbett & Keene
International Sales	The Sales Co
Insurance Services	Rollins Burdick Hunter
Completion Bond	The Completion Bond Company
Arriflex Camera & Cooke Lenses	Media Film Service, London
Lighting Equipment	Michael Samuelson Lighting
Grip Equipment	Grip House
Special Effects	Effects Associates
Titles	Frameline
Laboratory	Metrocolor
Film stock	Eastman Colour
Sound	Dolby SR
Original music composed by	David Motion
	Sally Potter
Additional material by	Fred Frith
	David Bedford
Music produced by	Bob Last
	David Motion
Music performed by:	
contra-bass clarinet	Richard Addison
violin, viola	Alexander Balanescu
violin	Clare Connors
bassoon	Lindsay Cooper
clarinets, saxophone	Andy Findon
guitars	Fred Frith

73

double bass	Christopher Laurence
keyboards	David Motion
trumpets, flugel horn	Bruce Nockles
voices	Sally Potter
	Jimmy Somerville

'Eliza is the Fairest Queen'
composed by
Edward Johnson
performed by
Jimmy Somerville
courtesy of London Records

'Where 'er You Walk'
composed by
George Frideric Handel
performed by
Andrew Watts
harpsichordist
Peter Hayward

'Coming'
composed by
Sally Potter, Jimmy Somerville, David Motion
published by
Copyright Control/Virgin Music
performed by
Jimmy Somerville
courtesy of London Records

for
Beatrice Quennell
'Hunny'
(1897–1989)

with special thanks to
Michael Powell
(1905–1990)

and thanks to

John Byrne	Caroline Potter
Alexandra Cann	Nicholas Quennell
Marilyn French	Andrei Razumovski
Renee Goddard	Yuri Romanenko
John Hargreaves	Christian Routh
Adrian Hodges	Charlotte Sheedy
Darragh Owens	Grace Tankersley
Angelo Pastore	Sergei Vronsky
Simon Perry	Kate Wilson

and to the town and people of Khiva, Uzbekhistan